THE VISUAL DICTIONARY *of*
SHIPS *and* SAILING

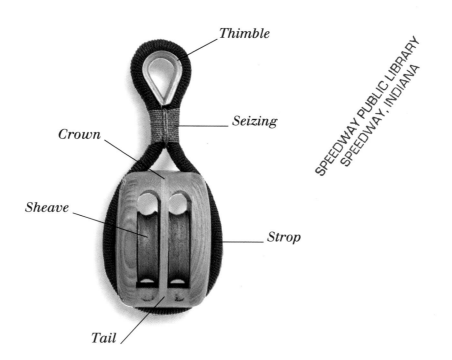

Thimble

Seizing

Crown

Sheave

Strop

Tail

A STROPPED BLOCK

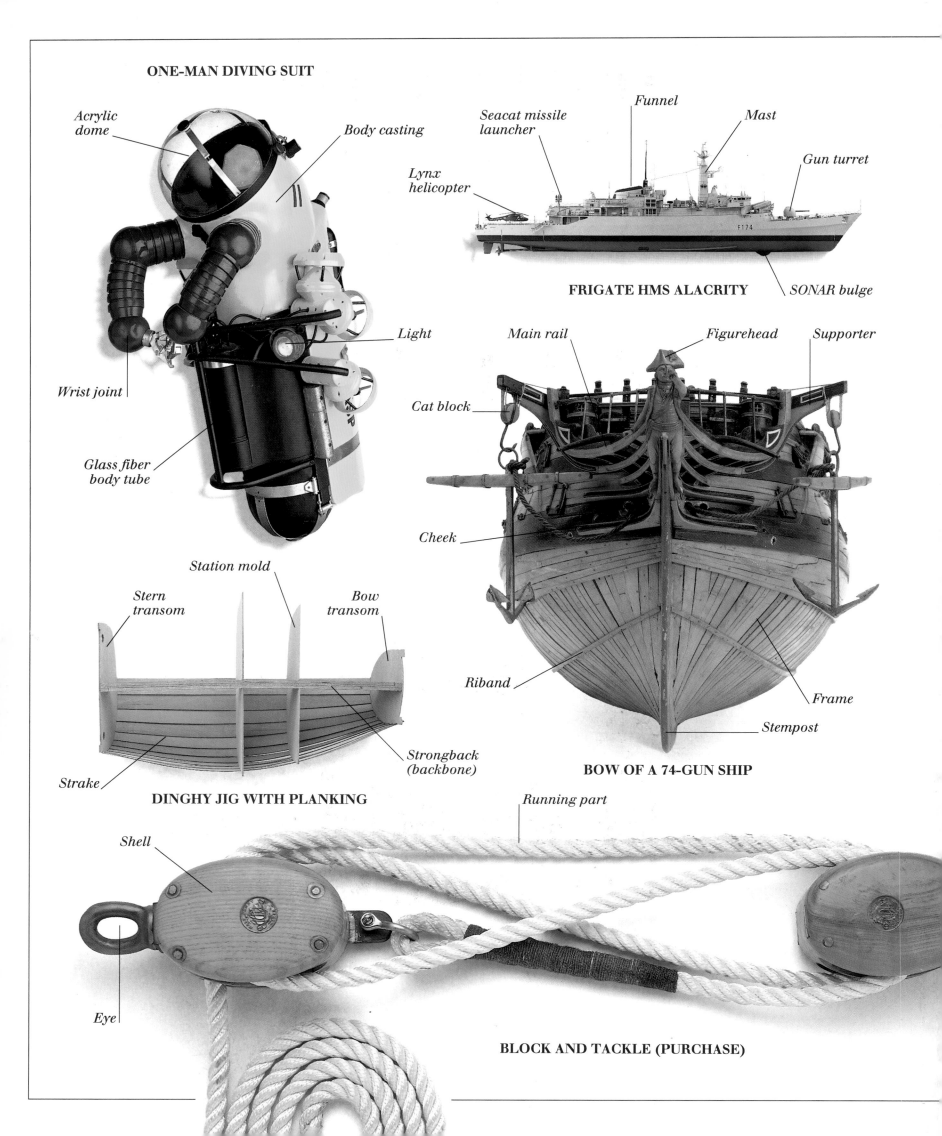

ONE-MAN DIVING SUIT

Acrylic dome

Body casting

Light

Wrist joint

Glass fiber body tube

FRIGATE HMS ALACRITY

Seacat missile launcher

Funnel

Mast

Gun turret

Lynx helicopter

SONAR bulge

F174

BOW OF A 74-GUN SHIP

Main rail

Figurehead

Supporter

Cat block

Cheek

Riband

Frame

Stempost

DINGHY JIG WITH PLANKING

Station mold

Stern transom

Bow transom

Strongback (backbone)

Strake

BLOCK AND TACKLE (PURCHASE)

Running part

Shell

Eye

EYEWITNESS VISUAL DICTIONARIES

THE VISUAL
DICTIONARY *of*
SHIPS *and*
SAILING

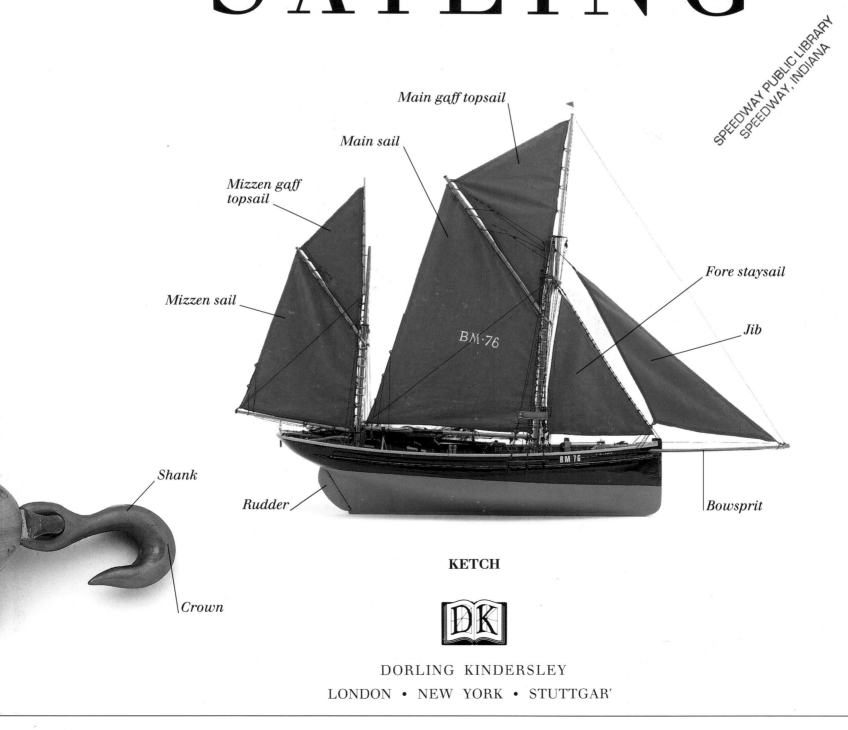

Main gaff topsail

Main sail

Mizzen gaff
topsail

Mizzen sail

Fore staysail

Jib

BM·76

BM 76

Shank

Rudder

Bowsprit

Crown

KETCH

DK

DORLING KINDERSLEY

LONDON • NEW YORK • STUTTGAR'

A DORLING KINDERSLEY BOOK

PROJECT ART EDITOR STEPHEN KNOWLDEN
DESIGN ASSISTANT PAUL CALVER

PROJECT EDITOR ROGER TRITTON

SERIES ART EDITOR PAUL WILKINSON
ART DIRECTOR CHEZ PICTHALL
MANAGING EDITOR RUTH MIDGLEY

CONSULTANT HARVEY B. LOOMIS

PHOTOGRAPHY JAMES STEVENSON, DAVE KING, STEVE GORTON, TIM RIDLEY

PRODUCTION HILARY STEPHENS

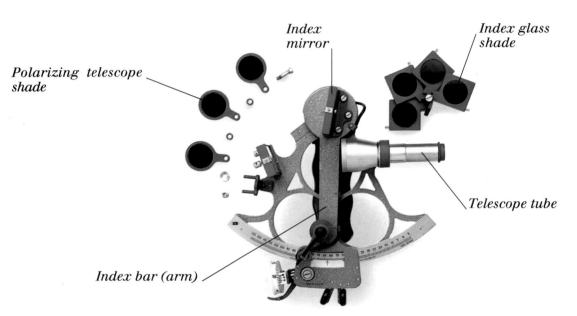

Index mirror

Index glass shade

Polarizing telescope shade

Telescope tube

Index bar (arm)

MODERN SEXTANT

FIRST AMERICAN EDITION, 1991

10 9 8 7 6 5 4 3

DORLING KINDERSLEY, INC., 232 MADISON AVENUE
NEW YORK, NEW YORK 10016

COPYRIGHT © 1991 DORLING KINDERSLEY LIMITED, LONDON

ISBN: 1-879431-20-3 (TRADE EDITION)
ISBN: 1-879431-35-1 (LIBRARY EDITION)

LIBRARY OF CONGRESS CARD CATALOG NUMBER: 91-060900

REPRODUCED BY GRB GRAFICA, VERONA, ITALY
PRINTED AND BOUND IN ITALY BY ARNOLDO MONDADORI, VERONA

Double rope becket

Sheave

Swallow

DUTCH TRIPLE FIDDLE BLOCK

Main sail

Jib

CHESAPEAKE BAY BATEAU

North cardinal point

Pivot

KELVIN LIGHT DRY COMPASS CARD

Pointed prow

Ambatch reed

Open stern

REED BOAT OF KENYA

Lugger topsail

Lug mainsail

LUGGER

Mile hand

Bezel

Base

PATENT LOG REGISTER

Contents

The first boats

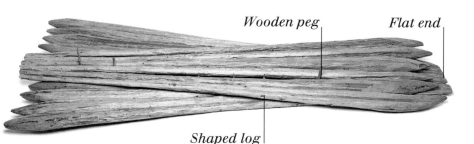

Wooden peg

Flat end

Shaped log

EARLY PEOPLE NEEDED BOATS TO TRAVEL, to trade and hunt, and to fish. They propelled their boats by hand, paddle, punting pole, or simple sail. Other than a floating tree trunk, man's first means of water transport was probably a raft. The Australian raft (right) could be built with the most elementary tools. Dugout logs and reeds—which are very light—were the materials most often used for early boats. The reed-built caballito was paddled through the surf of South American coastal waters, more like a float than a boat. The circular Iraqi guffa was used to carry cargo. It was simple to construct, and was often discarded once the journey was over. The guffa was made waterproof by being covered with pitch. By the third millenium B.C. the Egyptians were constructing sickle-shaped boats, like that at the bottom of the page, with cedar from Lebanon. The Egyptians also harnessed the wind with simple sails like that on the contemporary model of a traveling boat opposite. These boats were sailed from the Nile to trade with countries around the Mediterranean Sea.

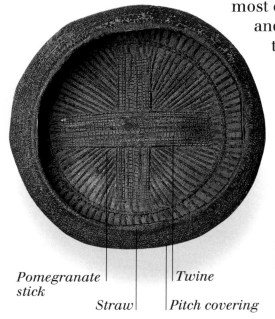

Pomegranate stick

Twine

Straw

Pitch covering

IRAQI GUFFA

Pointed prow

Scarfed joint

Built-up side

Dugout section

Ambatch reed

Tie

Square stern

Open stern

HAITIAN DUGOUT CANOE

REED BOAT OF KENYA

PERUVIAN CABALLITO (COASTAL REED BOAT)

Surf-riding prow

Cockpit

Bamboo reed

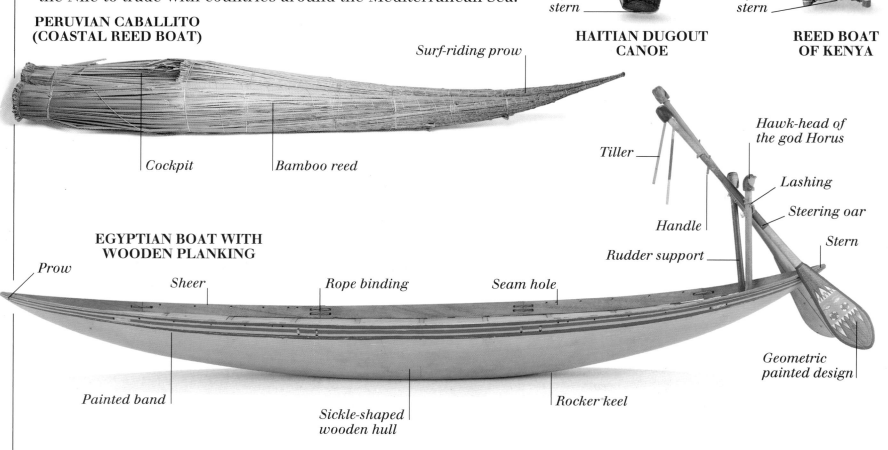

EGYPTIAN BOAT WITH WOODEN PLANKING

Tiller

Hawk-head of the god Horus

Lashing

Steering oar

Handle

Stern

Rudder support

Prow

Sheer

Rope binding

Seam hole

Geometric painted design

Painted band

Sickle-shaped wooden hull

Rocker keel

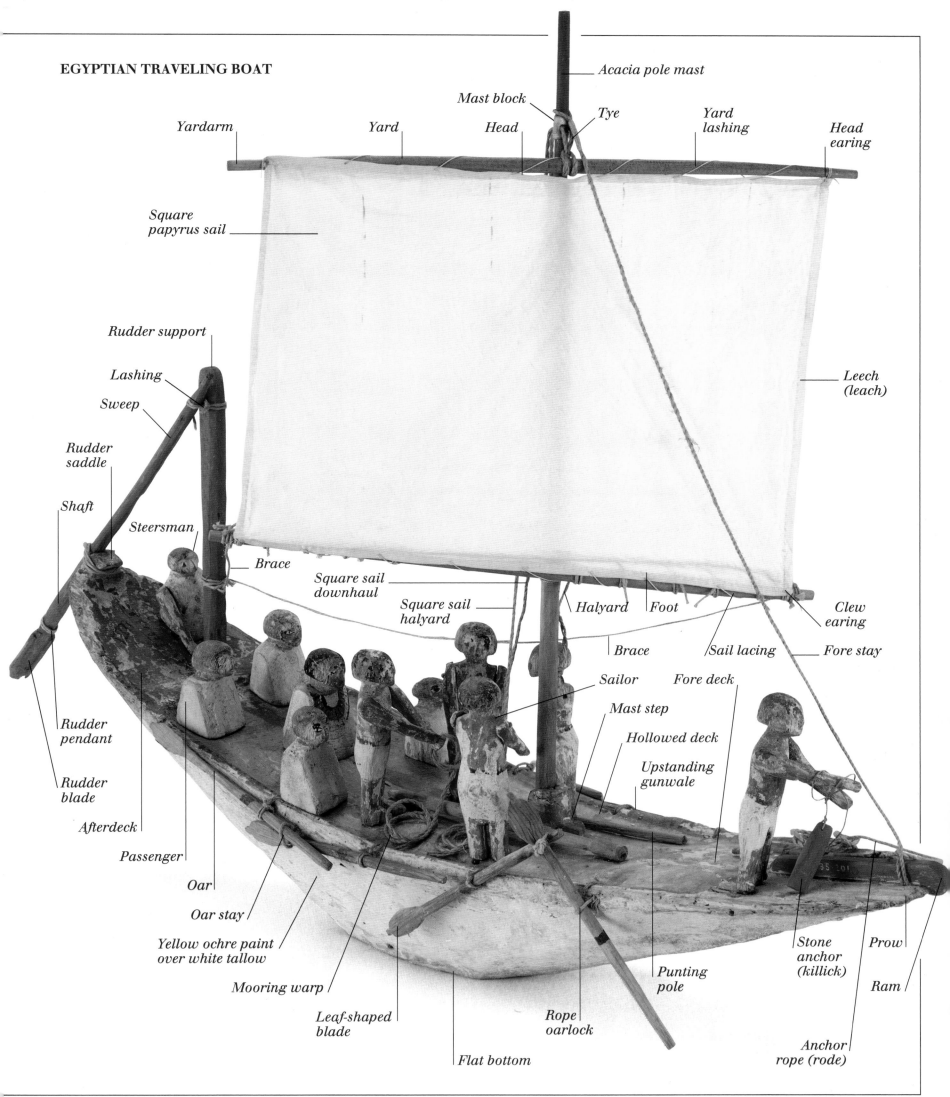

EGYPTIAN TRAVELING BOAT

Acacia pole mast

Mast block

Tye

Yardarm

Yard

Head

Yard lashing

Head earing

Square papyrus sail

Leech (leach)

Rudder support

Lashing

Sweep

Rudder saddle

Shaft

Steersman

Brace

Square sail downhaul

Square sail halyard

Halyard

Foot

Brace

Sail lacing

Clew earing

Fore stay

Sailor

Fore deck

Mast step

Hollowed deck

Rudder pendant

Upstanding gunwale

Rudder blade

Afterdeck

Passenger

Oar

Oar stay

Yellow ochre paint over white tallow

Mooring warp

Leaf-shaped blade

Flat bottom

Punting pole

Rope oarlock

Stone anchor (killick)

Prow

Ram

Anchor rope (rode)

Ships of Greece and Rome

ROMAN ANCHOR

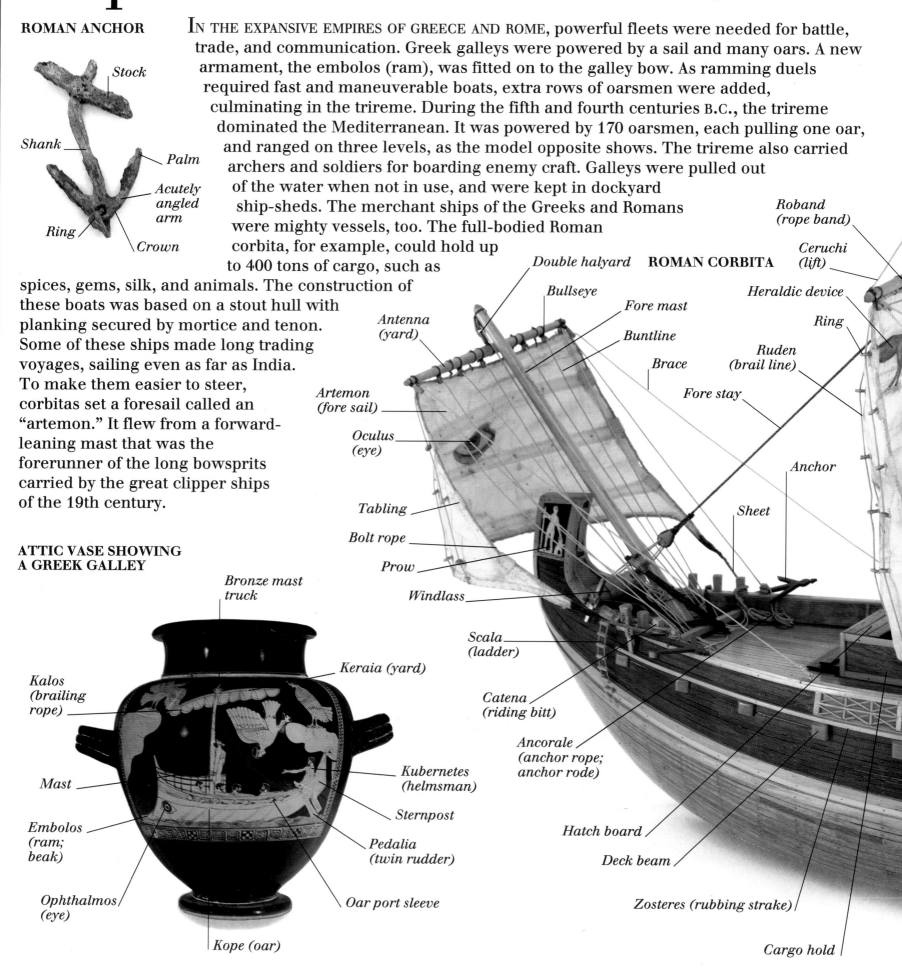

Stock

Shank

Palm

Acutely angled arm

Ring

Crown

IN THE EXPANSIVE EMPIRES OF GREECE AND ROME, powerful fleets were needed for battle, trade, and communication. Greek galleys were powered by a sail and many oars. A new armament, the embolos (ram), was fitted on to the galley bow. As ramming duels required fast and maneuverable boats, extra rows of oarsmen were added, culminating in the trireme. During the fifth and fourth centuries B.C., the trireme dominated the Mediterranean. It was powered by 170 oarsmen, each pulling one oar, and ranged on three levels, as the model opposite shows. The trireme also carried archers and soldiers for boarding enemy craft. Galleys were pulled out of the water when not in use, and were kept in dockyard ship-sheds. The merchant ships of the Greeks and Romans were mighty vessels, too. The full-bodied Roman corbita, for example, could hold up to 400 tons of cargo, such as spices, gems, silk, and animals. The construction of these boats was based on a stout hull with planking secured by mortice and tenon. Some of these ships made long trading voyages, sailing even as far as India. To make them easier to steer, corbitas set a foresail called an "artemon." It flew from a forward-leaning mast that was the forerunner of the long bowsprits carried by the great clipper ships of the 19th century.

ATTIC VASE SHOWING A GREEK GALLEY

Bronze mast truck

Kalos (brailing rope)

Keraia (yard)

Mast

Kubernetes (helmsman)

Embolos (ram; beak)

Sternpost

Pedalia (twin rudder)

Ophthalmos (eye)

Oar port sleeve

Kope (oar)

Roband (rope band)

Double halyard   **ROMAN CORBITA**

Bullseye

Ceruchi (lift)

Fore mast

Heraldic device

Antenna (yard)

Buntline

Ring

Brace

Ruden (brail line)

Artemon (fore sail)

Fore stay

Oculus (eye)

Anchor

Tabling

Sheet

Bolt rope

Prow

Windlass

Scala (ladder)

Catena (riding bitt)

Ancorale (anchor rope; anchor rode)

Hatch board

Deck beam

Zosteres (rubbing strake)

Cargo hold

8

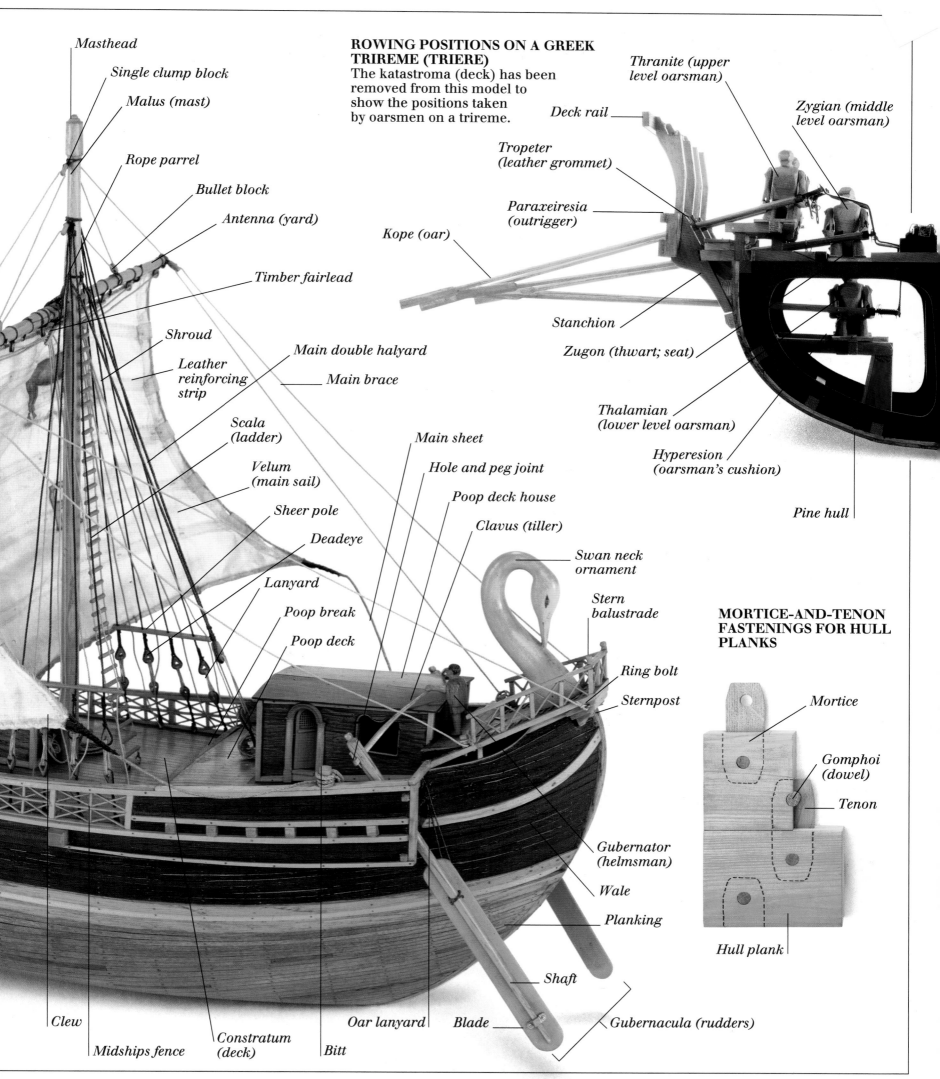

Masthead

Single clump block

Malus (mast)

Rope parrel

Bullet block

Antenna (yard)

Timber fairlead

Shroud

Leather
reinforcing
strip

Scala
(ladder)

Velum
(main sail)

Sheer pole

Deadeye

Lanyard

Poop break

Poop deck

Main double halyard

Main brace

Main sheet

Hole and peg joint

Poop deck house

Clavus (tiller)

Swan neck
ornament

Stern
balustrade

Ring bolt

Sternpost

Gubernator
(helmsman)

Wale

Planking

Clew

Midships fence

Constratum
(deck)

Bitt

Oar lanyard

Blade

Shaft

Gubernacula (rudders)

**ROWING POSITIONS ON A GREEK
TRIREME (TRIERE)**
The katastroma (deck) has been
removed from this model to
show the positions taken
by oarsmen on a trireme.

Thranite (upper
level oarsman)

Zygian (middle
level oarsman)

Deck rail

Tropeter
(leather grommet)

Paraxeiresia
(outrigger)

Kope (oar)

Stanchion

Zugon (thwart; seat)

Thalamian
(lower level oarsman)

Hyperesion
(oarsman's cushion)

Pine hull

**MORTICE-AND-TENON
FASTENINGS FOR HULL
PLANKS**

Mortice

Gomphoi
(dowel)

Tenon

Hull plank

9

Viking ships

In the dark ages (roughly 500 A.D. to 1000 A.D.) the longships of Scandinavia were among the most feared sights for people of northern Europe. The Vikings launched raids from Scandinavia every summer in longships equipped with a single steering oar on the right, or "steerboard" side (hence, "starboard"). A longboat had one row of oars on each side and a single sail. The hull was clinker-built, with overlapping planks. Prowheads adorned fighting ships during war campaigns. The longship was also used for coastal travel. The karv below was probably built as transport for an important family, while the smaller faering was a rowing boat only. The fleet of William of Normandy that invaded England in 1066 owed much to the Viking boat building tradition, and has been depicted in the Bayeux Tapestry (right). Seals of port towns and royal courts through the ages provide a record of contemporary ship design. The seal opposite shows a European craft from somewhat later than the Viking period. Fighting platforms, or castles, and the addition of more masts and sails changed the character of the medieval ship. Note also that the steering oar has been replaced by a centered rudder.

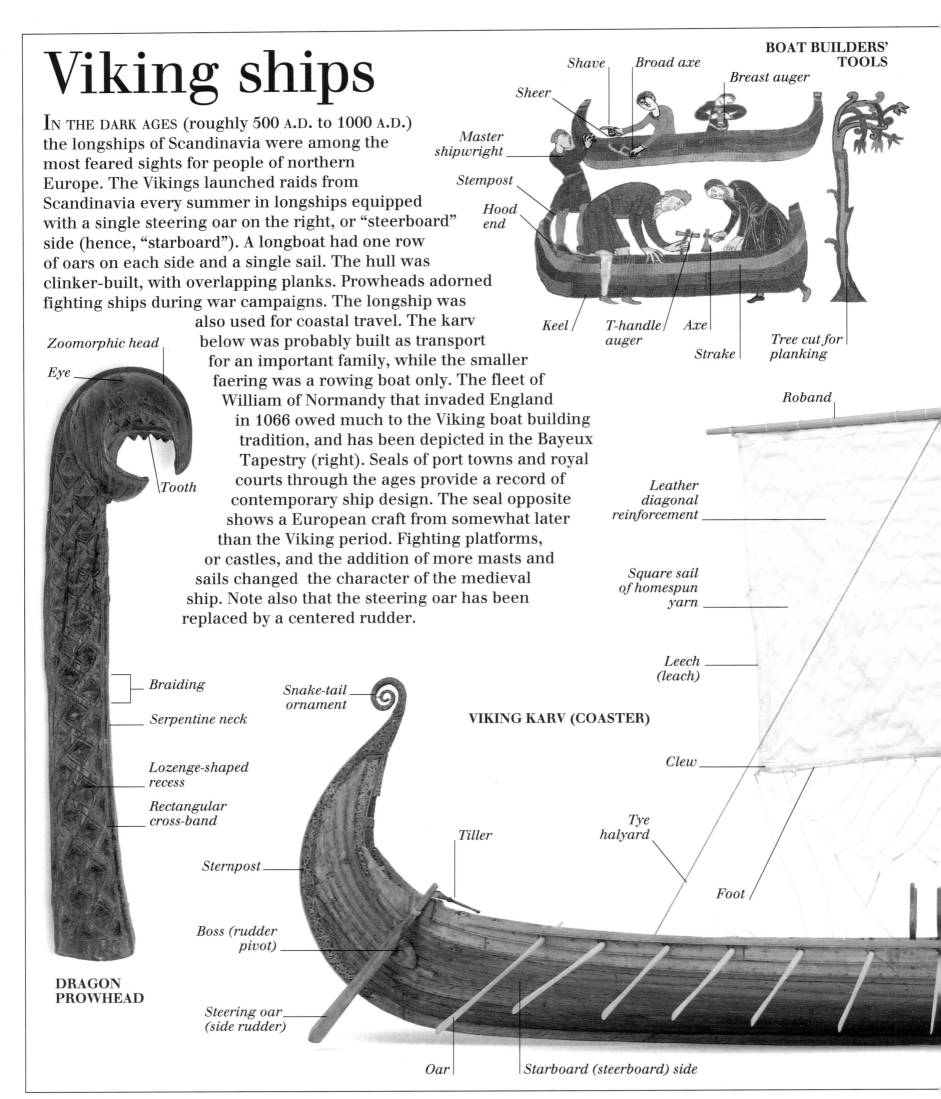

BOAT BUILDERS' TOOLS

Shave

Broad axe

Breast auger

Sheer

Master shipwright

Stempost

Hood end

Keel

T-handle auger

Axe

Strake

Tree cut for planking

Zoomorphic head

Eye

Tooth

Braiding

Serpentine neck

Lozenge-shaped recess

Rectangular cross-band

DRAGON PROWHEAD

Snake-tail ornament

VIKING KARV (COASTER)

Sternpost

Boss (rudder pivot)

Steering oar (side rudder)

Tiller

Oar

Starboard (steerboard) side

Roband

Leather diagonal reinforcement

Square sail of homespun yarn

Leech (leach)

Clew

Tye halyard

Foot

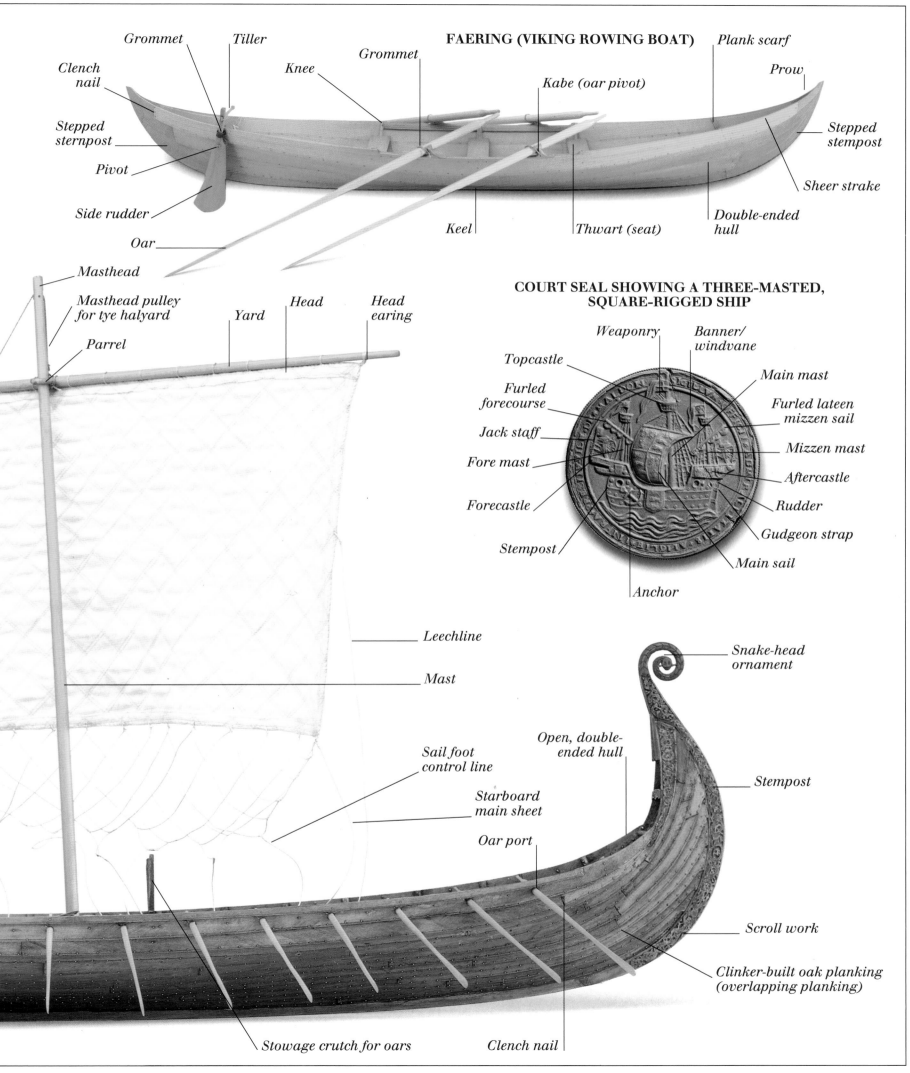

FAERING (VIKING ROWING BOAT)

Grommet

Tiller

Clench nail

Knee

Grommet

Plank scarf

Prow

Kabe (oar pivot)

Stepped sternpost

Stepped stempost

Pivot

Side rudder

Sheer strake

Oar

Keel

Thwart (seat)

Double-ended hull

Masthead

Masthead pulley for tye halyard

Yard

Head

Head earing

Parrel

COURT SEAL SHOWING A THREE-MASTED, SQUARE-RIGGED SHIP

Weaponry

Banner/ windvane

Topcastle

Main mast

Furled forecourse

Furled lateen mizzen sail

Jack staff

Mizzen mast

Fore mast

Aftercastle

Forecastle

Rudder

Gudgeon strap

Stempost

Main sail

Anchor

Leechline

Mast

Snake-head ornament

Open, double-ended hull

Sail foot control line

Stempost

Starboard main sheet

Oar port

Scroll work

Clinker-built oak planking (overlapping planking)

Stowage crutch for oars

Clench nail

11

Ships for war and trade

FROM THE 16TH CENTURY, SHIPS WERE BUILT WITH A NEW FORM OF HULL, constructed with carvel (edge-to-edge) planking. Warships of the time, like King Henry VIII of England's Mary Rose, boasted awesome fire power. This ship carried both long-range bronze cannon, and short-range, anti personnel guns in iron. Elsewhere, ships took on a multiformity of shapes. Dhows transported slaves from East Africa to Arabia, their fore-and-aft rigged lateen sails allowing them to sail close to the wind around the lands of the Indian Ocean. The Chinese sailed to East Africa and Arabia in junks, trading goods that were carried in watertight compartments. New astronomical tools helped medieval sailors to find their way. Cross-staves and astrolabes were used to measure the altitude of the sun or stars. One of the cross-pieces was slid along the staff of the cross-stave—which was graduated in degrees of altitude—until its top aligned with the celestial body and its base with the horizon. The sighting rule of the astrolabe was simply lined up with a known body, and its altitude read from marks on the metal disk. Sundials used the shadow of the sun to show sailors the time of day.

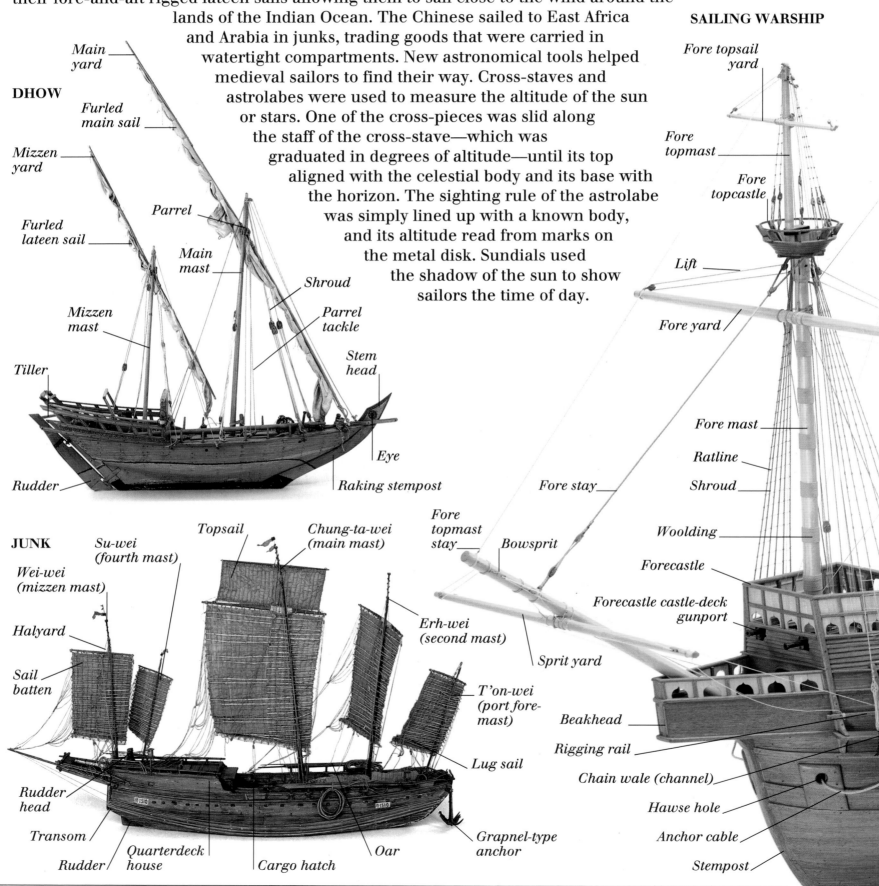

DHOW

Main yard
Furled main sail
Mizzen yard
Furled lateen sail
Parrel
Main mast
Mizzen mast
Shroud
Parrel tackle
Stem head
Tiller
Rudder
Eye
Raking stempost

JUNK

Su-wei (fourth mast)
Wei-wei (mizzen mast)
Halyard
Sail batten
Rudder head
Transom
Rudder
Quarterdeck house
Topsail
Chung-ta-wei (main mast)
Erh-wei (second mast)
T'on-wei (port fore-mast)
Lug sail
Cargo hatch
Oar
Grapnel-type anchor

SAILING WARSHIP

Fore topsail yard
Fore topmast
Fore topcastle
Lift
Fore yard
Fore mast
Ratline
Shroud
Woolding
Forecastle
Forecastle castle-deck gunport
Fore stay
Fore topmast stay
Bowsprit
Sprit yard
Beakhead
Rigging rail
Chain wale (channel)
Hawse hole
Anchor cable
Stempost

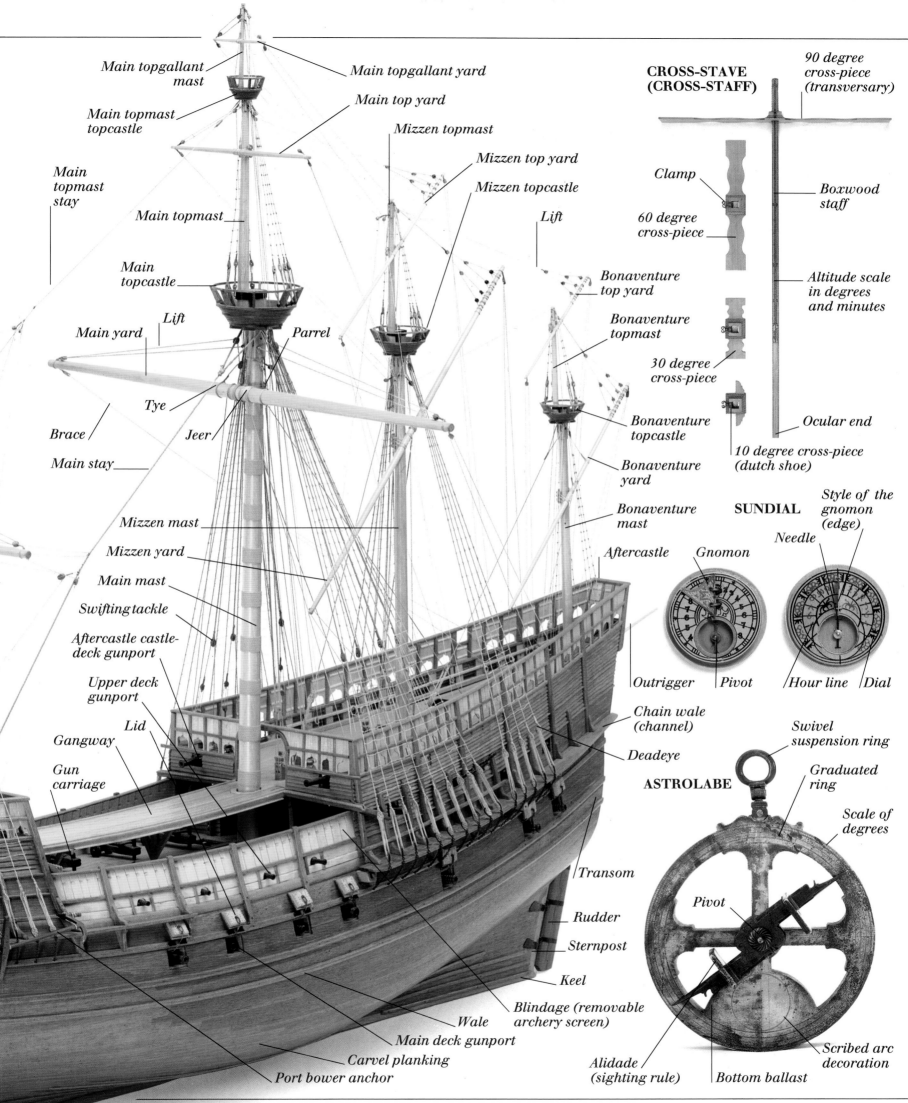

Main topgallant mast

Main topgallant yard

Main topmast topcastle

Main top yard

Mizzen topmast

Main topmast stay

Mizzen top yard

Main topmast

Mizzen topcastle

Lift

Main topcastle

Bonaventure top yard

Lift

Bonaventure topmast

Main yard

Parrel

Tye

Bonaventure topcastle

Jeer

Brace

Bonaventure yard

Main stay

Bonaventure mast

Mizzen mast

Aftercastle

Mizzen yard

Main mast

Swifting tackle

Aftercastle castle-deck gunport

Upper deck gunport

Outrigger   Pivot

Hour line   Dial

Lid

Chain wale (channel)

Gangway

Deadeye

Gun carriage

Transom

Rudder

Sternpost

Keel

Wale

Blindage (removable archery screen)

Main deck gunport

Carvel planking

Port bower anchor

CROSS-STAVE (CROSS-STAFF)

90 degree cross-piece (transversary)

Clamp

Boxwood staff

60 degree cross-piece

Altitude scale in degrees and minutes

30 degree cross-piece

Ocular end

10 degree cross-piece (dutch shoe)

SUNDIAL

Style of the gnomon (edge)

Needle

Gnomon

ASTROLABE

Swivel suspension ring

Graduated ring

Scale of degrees

Pivot

Alidade (sighting rule)

Bottom ballast

Scribed arc decoration

13

The expansion of sail

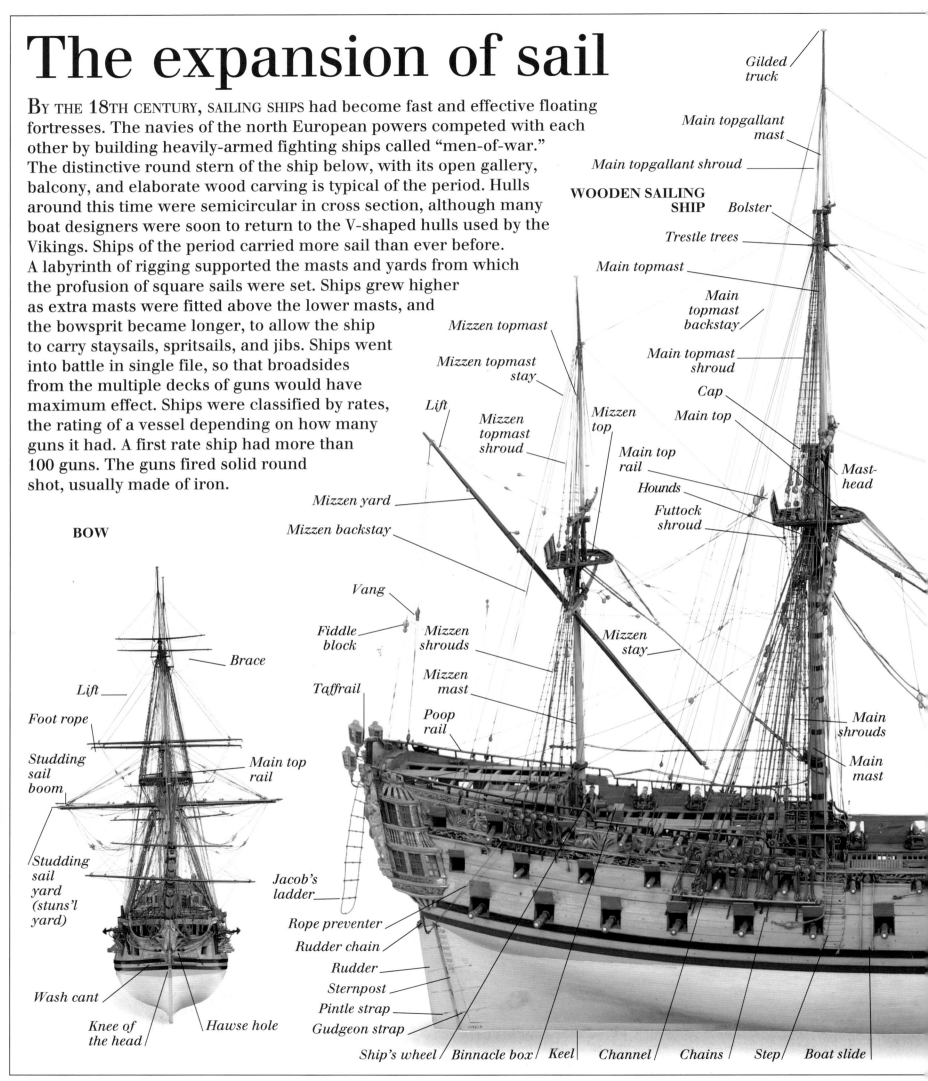

By THE 18TH CENTURY, SAILING SHIPS had become fast and effective floating fortresses. The navies of the north European powers competed with each other by building heavily-armed fighting ships called "men-of-war." The distinctive round stern of the ship below, with its open gallery, balcony, and elaborate wood carving is typical of the period. Hulls around this time were semicircular in cross section, although many boat designers were soon to return to the V-shaped hulls used by the Vikings. Ships of the period carried more sail than ever before. A labyrinth of rigging supported the masts and yards from which the profusion of square sails were set. Ships grew higher as extra masts were fitted above the lower masts, and the bowsprit became longer, to allow the ship to carry staysails, spritsails, and jibs. Ships went into battle in single file, so that broadsides from the multiple decks of guns would have maximum effect. Ships were classified by rates, the rating of a vessel depending on how many guns it had. A first rate ship had more than 100 guns. The guns fired solid round shot, usually made of iron.

Gilded truck

Main topgallant mast

Main topgallant shroud

WOODEN SAILING SHIP

Bolster

Trestle trees

Main topmast

Main topmast backstay

Main topmast shroud

Cap

Main top

Mizzen topmast

Mizzen topmast stay

Lift

Mizzen topmast shroud

Mizzen top

Main top rail

Masthead

Hounds

Futtock shroud

Mizzen yard

Mizzen backstay

BOW

Vang

Fiddle block

Mizzen shrouds

Mizzen stay

Brace

Lift

Foot rope

Taffrail

Mizzen mast

Poop rail

Main shrouds

Main mast

Studding sail boom

Main top rail

Studding sail yard (stuns'l yard)

Jacob's ladder

Rope preventer

Rudder chain

Rudder

Sternpost

Pintle strap

Gudgeon strap

Wash cant

Knee of the head

Hawse hole

Ship's wheel

Binnacle box

Keel

Channel

Chains

Step

Boat slide

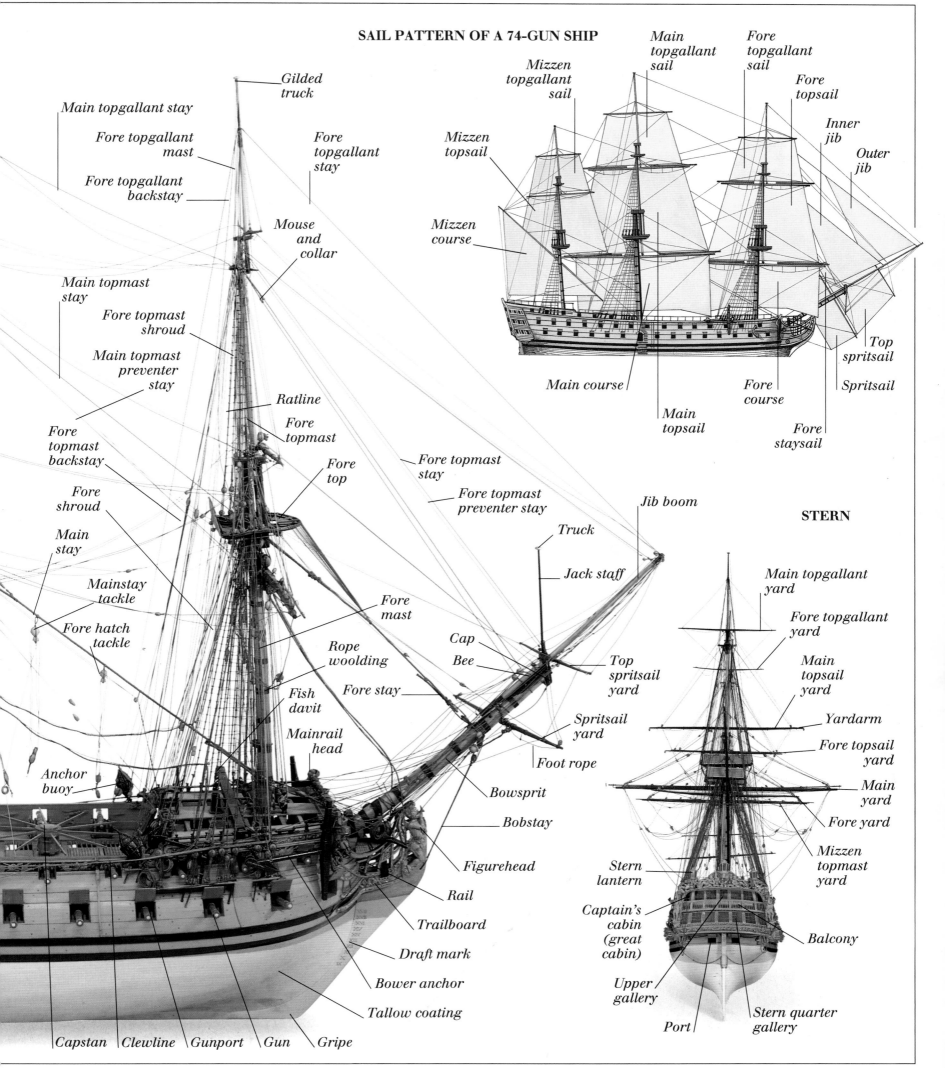

SAIL PATTERN OF A 74-GUN SHIP

Gilded truck

Main topgallant stay

Fore topgallant mast

Fore topgallant backstay

Fore topgallant stay

Mouse and collar

Main topmast stay

Fore topmast shroud

Main topmast preventer stay

Ratline

Fore topmast

Fore top

Fore topmast stay

Fore topmast preventer stay

Fore topmast backstay

Fore shroud

Main stay

Mainstay tackle

Fore hatch tackle

Mizzen topgallant sail

Mizzen topsail

Mizzen course

Main topgallant sail

Fore topgallant sail

Fore topgallant sail

Fore topsail

Inner jib

Outer jib

Top spritsail

Spritsail

Main course

Main topsail

Fore course

Fore staysail

Jib boom

Truck

Jack staff

STERN

Main topgallant yard

Fore topgallant yard

Main topsail yard

Yardarm

Fore topsail yard

Main yard

Fore yard

Mizzen topmast yard

Cap

Bee

Top spritsail yard

Spritsail yard

Foot rope

Rope woolding

Fore stay

Fish davit

Mainrail head

Bowsprit

Bobstay

Figurehead

Anchor buoy

Rail

Trailboard

Draft mark

Bower anchor

Tallow coating

Capstan   Clewline   Gunport   Gun   Gripe

Stern lantern

Captain's cabin (great cabin)

Upper gallery

Port

Stern quarter gallery

Balcony

15

A ship of the line

THE 74-GUN THIRD-RATER WAS A MAINSTAY of British and French battlefleets in the late 18th and early 19th centuries. (The biggest ships in the fledgling American navy of the time were 44-gun frigates.) The length of such a man-of-war was determined by the number of guns needed for each deck, allowing room for crews to man them. The gun deck of this vessel was about 170 ft (52 m) long. Her decks had to be strong to carry the weight of the guns. The deck planks have been removed in the model below to illustrate the number of beams needed to make the hull strong enough. Only timber with perfect grain was used. The upper deck was open at the waist, but forward and aft were officers' cabins. The forecastle (foc's'l) and quarterdeck carried light guns and provided platforms for handling the rigging and for reconnaissance. The ship's longboats, or launches, were carried on skids between the gangways.

LONGBOAT

UPPER DECK OF A 74-GUN SHIP

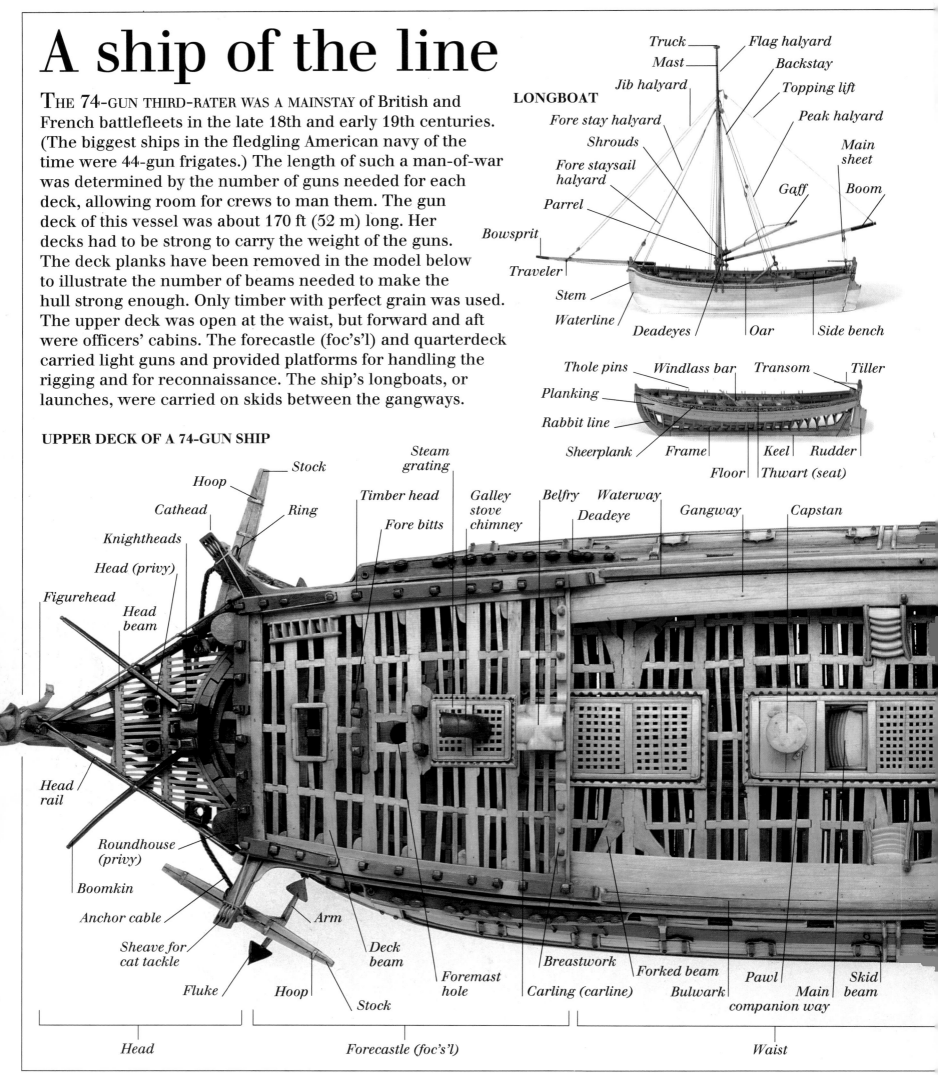

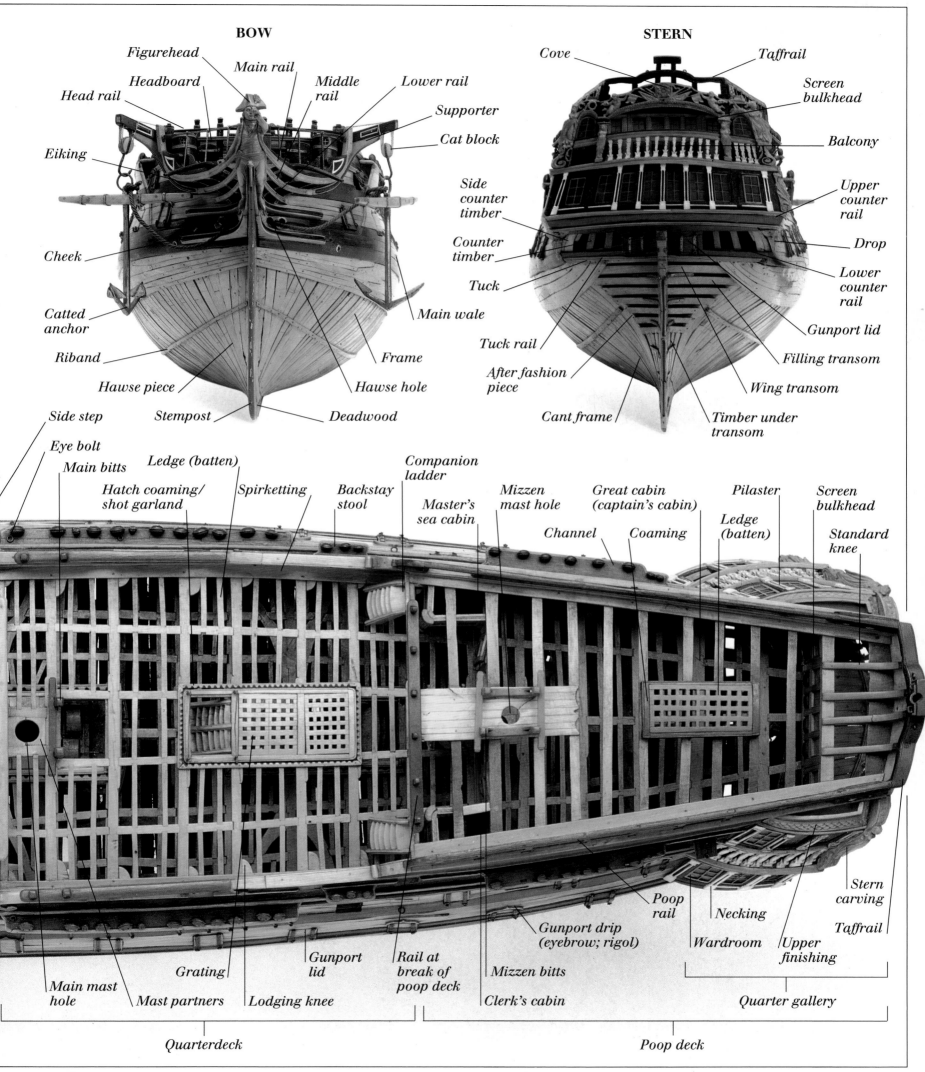

BOW

Figurehead

Main rail

Headboard

Middle rail

Lower rail

Head rail

Supporter

Cat block

Eiking

Cheek

Catted anchor

Riband

Main wale

Hawse piece

Frame

Stempost

Deadwood

Hawse hole

STERN

Cove

Taffrail

Screen bulkhead

Balcony

Side counter timber

Upper counter rail

Counter timber

Drop

Tuck

Lower counter rail

Gunport lid

Tuck rail

Filling transom

After fashion piece

Wing transom

Cant frame

Timber under transom

Side step

Eye bolt

Main bitts

Ledge (batten)

Companion ladder

Mizzen mast hole

Great cabin (captain's cabin)

Pilaster

Screen bulkhead

Hatch coaming/ shot garland

Spirketting

Backstay stool

Master's sea cabin

Channel

Coaming

Ledge (batten)

Standard knee

Main mast hole

Mast partners

Grating

Lodging knee

Gunport lid

Rail at break of poop deck

Mizzen bitts

Clerk's cabin

Gunport drip (eyebrow; rigol)

Poop rail

Necking

Wardroom

Upper finishing

Stern carving

Taffrail

Quarter gallery

Quarterdeck

Poop deck

17

Anatomy of a wooden ship

THE SKELETON OF A WOODEN SHIP is a complex system of timbers joined together to form the frame, on which the planks and decks are attached. The many parts of a man-of-war's frame are laid out flat below to show the shape of each unit. (The old-fashioned terms for each piece of the frame are given.) The completed frame of a smaller craft, a collier brig, is shown opposite. Ship builders used wood from specially grown trees called "grown oaks" (right), whose limbs conformed naturally to the shapes needed for the knees, ryders, and other pieces that make up the frame. Water and heat were used to bend the oak to the final fit.

GROWN OAKS (COMPASS TIMBERS)

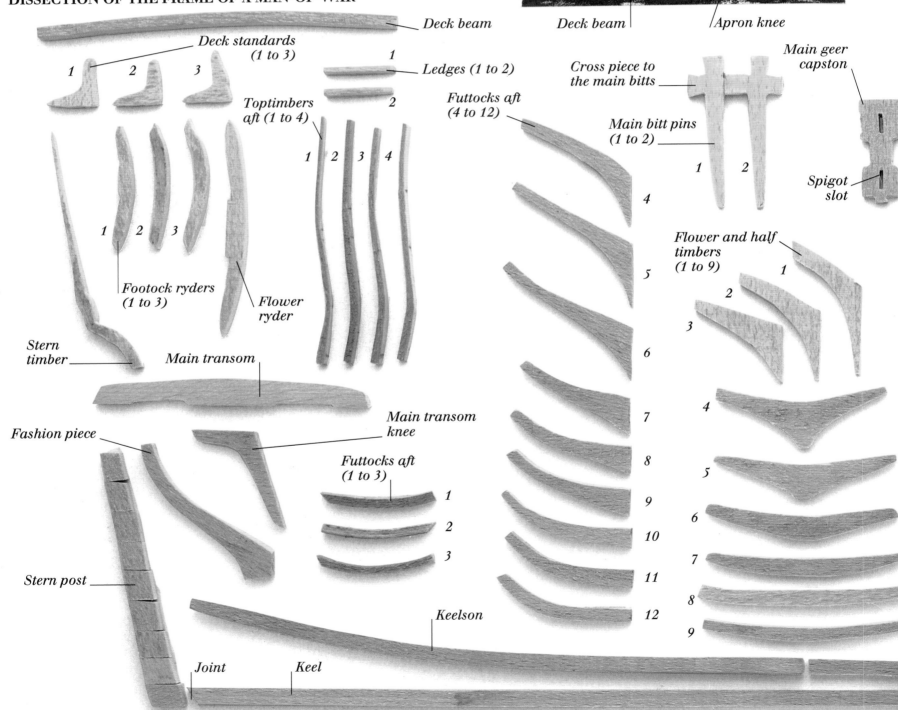

Ryder

Knee

Oak tree

Deck beam

Apron knee

DISSECTION OF THE FRAME OF A MAN-OF-WAR

Deck beam

Deck standards (1 to 3)

1   2   3

1

Ledges (1 to 2)

2

Toptimbers aft (1 to 4)

1   2   3   4

1   2   3

Footock ryders (1 to 3)

Flower ryder

Stern timber

Main transom

Fashion piece

Main transom knee

Futtocks aft (1 to 3)

1

2

3

Stern post

Joint

Keel

Futtocks aft (4 to 12)

4

5

6

7

8

9

10

11

12

Keelson

Cross piece to the main bitts

Main bitt pins (1 to 2)

1   2

Main geer capston

Spigot slot

Flower and half timbers (1 to 9)

1

2

3

4

5

6

7

8

9

18

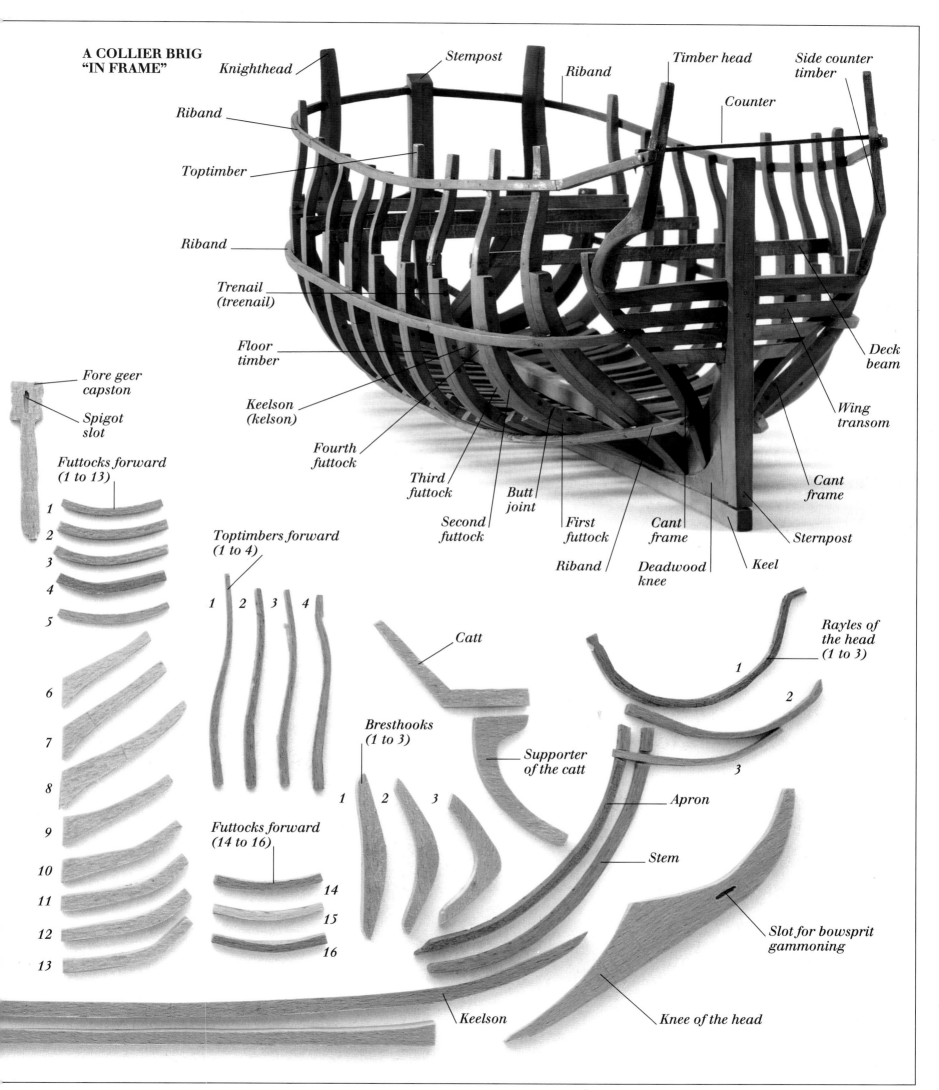

A COLLIER BRIG "IN FRAME"

Knighthead

Stempost

Riband

Timber head

Side counter timber

Riband

Counter

Toptimber

Riband

Trenail (treenail)

Floor timber

Deck beam

Fore geer capston

Keelson (kelson)

Wing transom

Spigot slot

Fourth futtock

Cant frame

Futtocks forward (1 to 13)

Third futtock

Butt joint

First futtock

Cant frame

Sternpost

Second futtock

Cant frame

Keel

1

2

3

4

5

6

7

8

9

10

11

12

13

Toptimbers forward (1 to 4)

1 2 3 4

Catt

Riband

Deadwood knee

Keel

Rayles of the head (1 to 3)

1

2

Bresthooks (1 to 3)

Supporter of the catt

3

Futtocks forward (14 to 16)

1 2 3

Apron

Stem

14

15

16

Slot for bowsprit gammoning

Keelson

Knee of the head

Anatomy of an iron ship

IRON PARTS WERE USED IN WOODEN SHIPS AS EARLY AS 1675, often in the same form as the wooden parts that they replaced. Eventually, as on the tea clipper Cutty Sark (below), iron standing rigging was found to be stronger than the traditional rope. The first "ironclads" were warships whose wooden hulls were protected by iron armor plates. Later ironclads actually had iron hulls. The model opposite is based on the British warship HMS Warrior, launched in 1860, the first battleship built entirely of iron. The plan of an iron paddlesteamer (bottom), built somewhat later, shows that the craft had the masts and bowsprit of a sailing ship; but it also boasted a steam propulsion plant amidships that turned two side paddlewheels. Early iron plates were painstakingly riveted together (below), but by the 1940s, steel vessels were welded together, whole sections at a time. The Liberty ships built in America during World War II are prime examples of such "production-line" vessels.

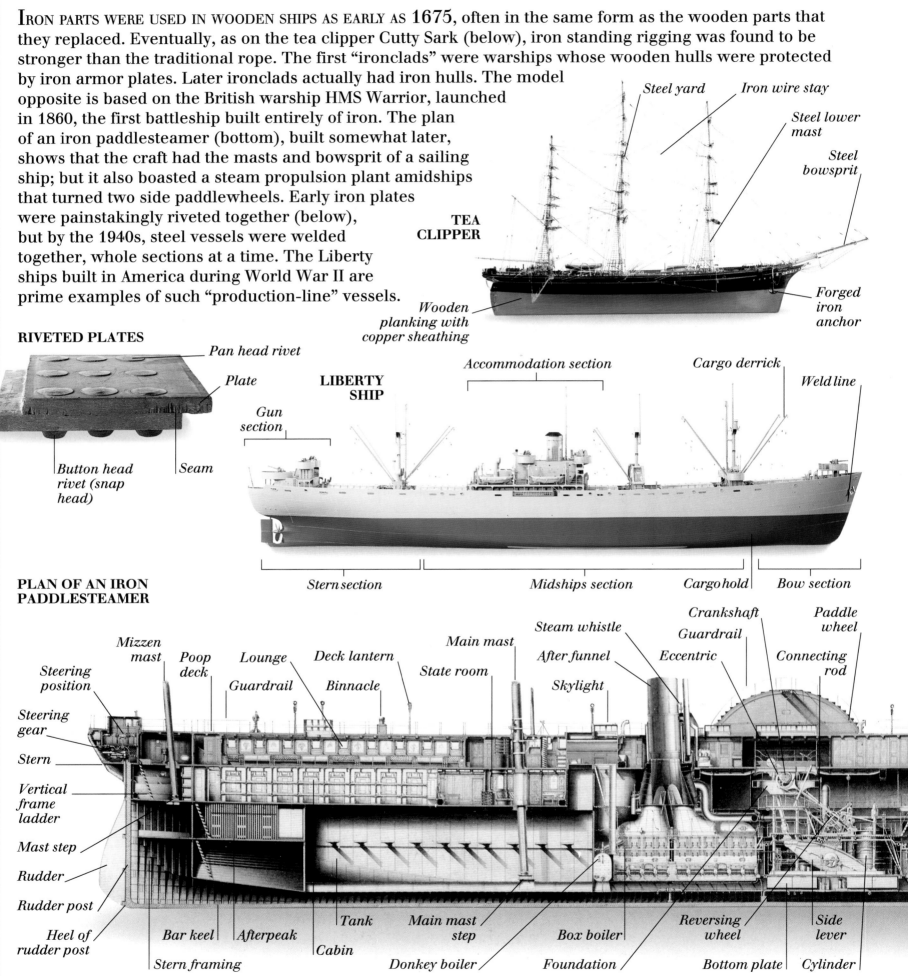

TEA CLIPPER

Steel yard

Iron wire stay

Steel lower mast

Steel bowsprit

Forged iron anchor

Wooden planking with copper sheathing

RIVETED PLATES

Pan head rivet

Plate

Button head rivet (snap head)

Seam

LIBERTY SHIP

Accommodation section

Cargo derrick

Weld line

Gun section

Stern section

Midships section

Cargo hold

Bow section

PLAN OF AN IRON PADDLESTEAMER

Mizzen mast

Poop deck

Lounge

Deck lantern

Main mast

Steam whistle

Crankshaft

Paddle wheel

Guardrail

Connecting rod

After funnel

Eccentric

Steering position

Guardrail

Binnacle

State room

Skylight

Steering gear

Stern

Vertical frame ladder

Mast step

Rudder

Rudder post

Heel of rudder post

Bar keel

Afterpeak

Cabin

Tank

Main mast step

Donkey boiler

Box boiler

Foundation

Reversing wheel

Bottom plate

Side lever

Cylinder

Stern framing

20

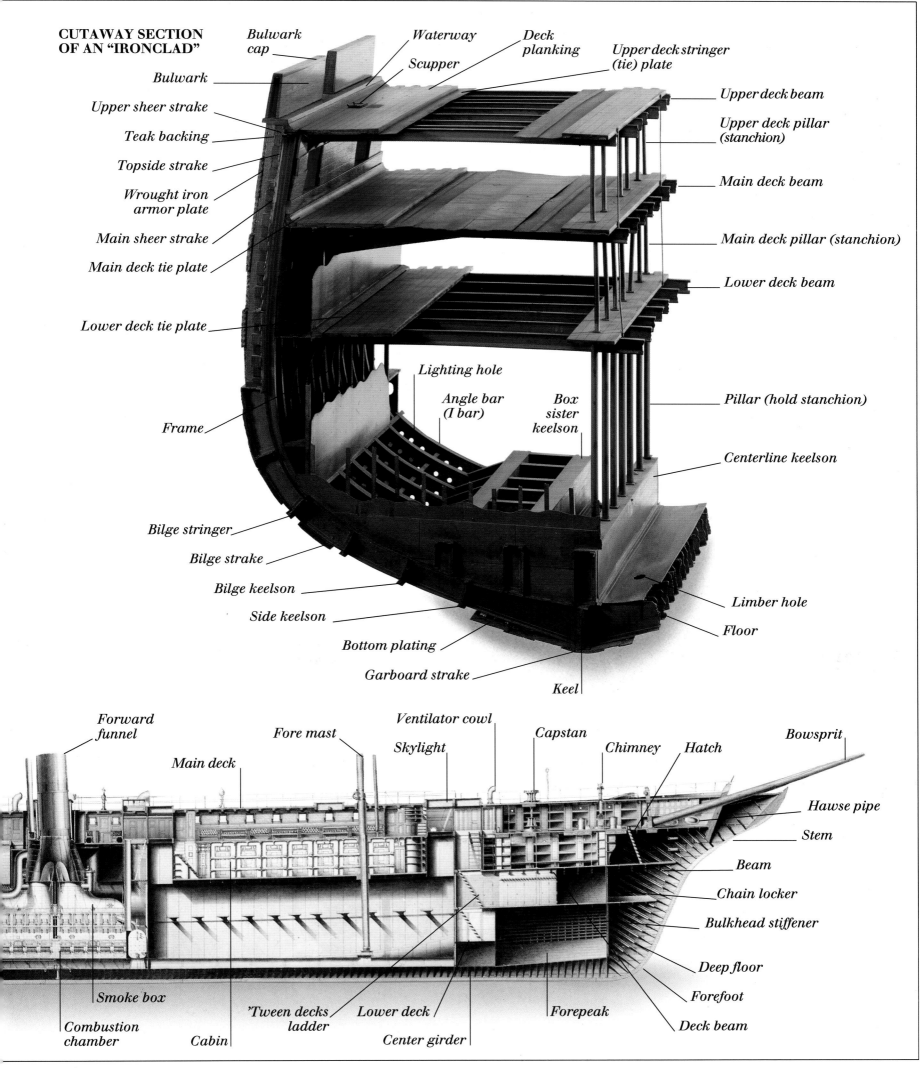

CUTAWAY SECTION OF AN "IRONCLAD"

Bulwark cap

Waterway

Deck planking

Upper deck stringer (tie) plate

Bulwark

Scupper

Upper deck beam

Upper sheer strake

Upper deck pillar (stanchion)

Teak backing

Topside strake

Main deck beam

Wrought iron armor plate

Main sheer strake

Main deck pillar (stanchion)

Main deck tie plate

Lower deck beam

Lower deck tie plate

Lighting hole

Angle bar (I bar)

Box sister keelson

Pillar (hold stanchion)

Frame

Centerline keelson

Bilge stringer

Bilge strake

Bilge keelson

Limber hole

Side keelson

Floor

Bottom plating

Garboard strake

Keel

Forward funnel

Ventilator cowl

Capstan

Bowsprit

Fore mast

Skylight

Chimney

Hatch

Main deck

Hawse pipe

Stem

Beam

Chain locker

Bulkhead stiffener

Smoke box

'Tween decks ladder

Lower deck

Forepeak

Deep floor

Combustion chamber

Cabin

Center girder

Forefoot

Deck beam

21

Paddle wheels and propellers

THE INVENTION OF THE STEAM ENGINE IN THE 18TH CENTURY made mechanically driven ships fitted with paddle wheels or propellers a viable alternative to sails. Paddle wheels have fixed or feathered floats, and the model shown below features both types. Feathered floats give more propulsive power than fixed floats because they are almost upright at all times in the water. Paddle wheels were superseded by the propeller on oceangoing vessels in the mid-19th century. Propellers are more efficient, work better in rough water, and are less vulnerable in collisions. The first propellers were two-bladed, but later three- and four-bladed versions are more powerful; the shape and pitch of the blades have also been refined over the years. At the beginning of the 18th century, tillers were replaced on many larger ships by the ship's wheel as a means of steering.

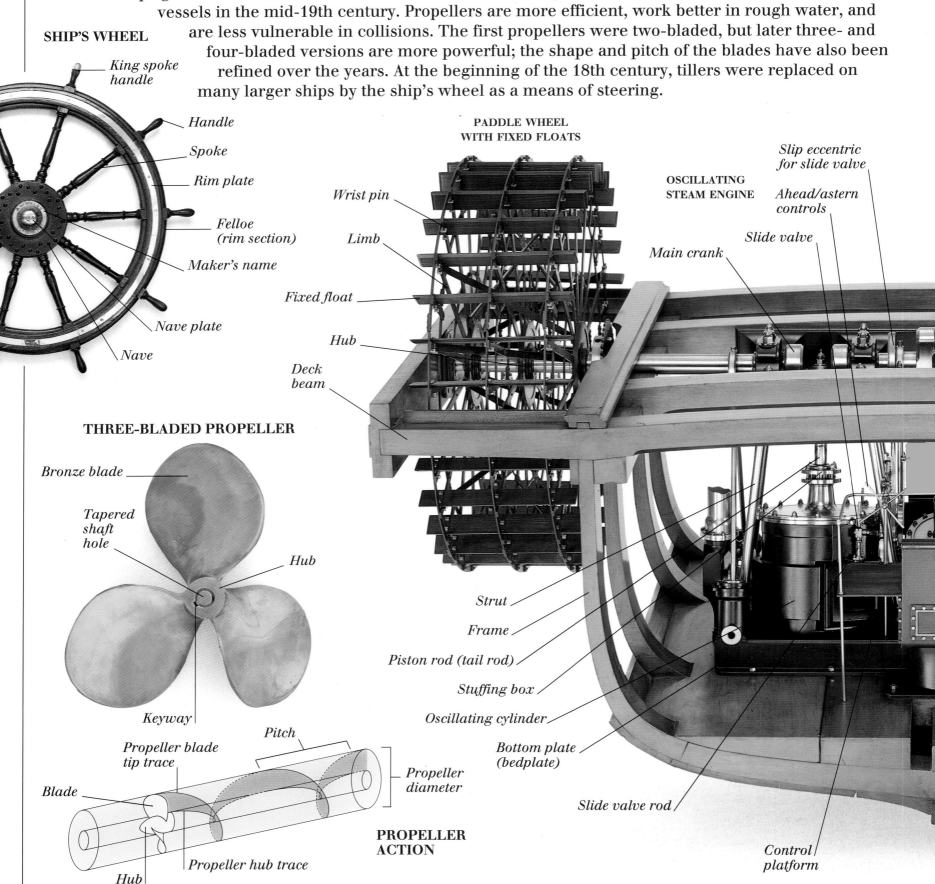

SHIP'S WHEEL

King spoke handle

Handle

Spoke

Rim plate

Felloe (rim section)

Maker's name

Nave plate

Nave

PADDLE WHEEL WITH FIXED FLOATS

Wrist pin

Limb

Fixed float

Hub

Deck beam

OSCILLATING STEAM ENGINE

Slip eccentric for slide valve

Ahead/astern controls

Slide valve

Main crank

THREE-BLADED PROPELLER

Bronze blade

Tapered shaft hole

Hub

Keyway

Strut

Frame

Piston rod (tail rod)

Stuffing box

Oscillating cylinder

Bottom plate (bedplate)

Slide valve rod

Control platform

Pitch

Propeller blade tip trace

Blade

Propeller diameter

Propeller hub trace

Hub

PROPELLER ACTION

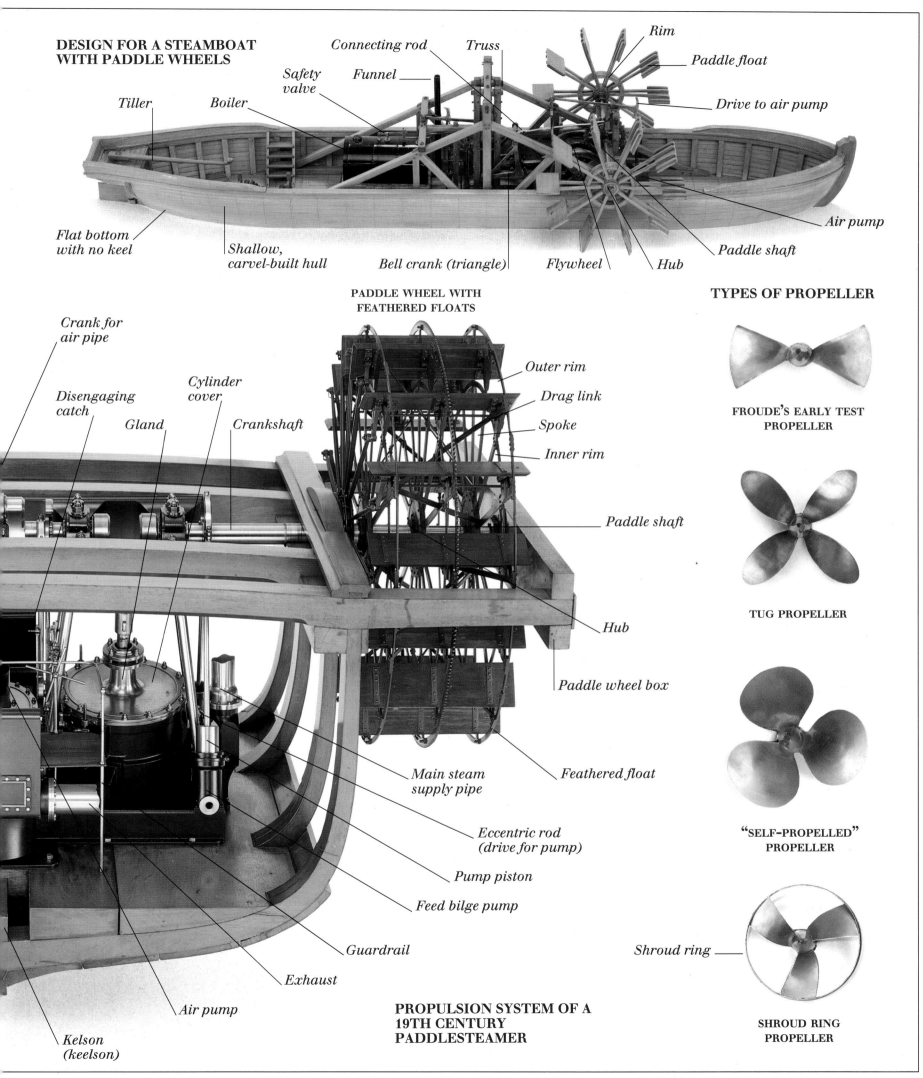

DESIGN FOR A STEAMBOAT WITH PADDLE WHEELS

Connecting rod

Truss

Rim

Paddle float

Safety valve

Funnel

Tiller

Boiler

Drive to air pump

Flat bottom with no keel

Shallow, carvel-built hull

Bell crank (triangle)

Flywheel

Hub

Paddle shaft

Air pump

PADDLE WHEEL WITH FEATHERED FLOATS

TYPES OF PROPELLER

Crank for air pipe

Disengaging catch

Gland

Cylinder cover

Crankshaft

Outer rim

Drag link

Spoke

Inner rim

Paddle shaft

Hub

Paddle wheel box

Main steam supply pipe

Feathered float

Eccentric rod (drive for pump)

Pump piston

Feed bilge pump

Guardrail

Exhaust

Air pump

Kelson (keelson)

FROUDE'S EARLY TEST PROPELLER

TUG PROPELLER

"SELF-PROPELLED" PROPELLER

Shroud ring

SHROUD RING PROPELLER

PROPULSION SYSTEM OF A 19TH CENTURY PADDLESTEAMER

The boat builder's yard

TRADITIONALLY, MOST SMALL BOATS were built in a painstaking way by softening and shaping tropical hardwoods, and by fastening the planks (strakes) with copper rivets. Modern boats, in contrast, are often built of plywood or fiberglass, with epoxy resin glues, and synthetic rope and sail cloth. The 7 ft 6 in (2.3 m) marine plywood dinghy shown here, with its flat pram bow, is clinker-built—that is, built with overlapping strakes. It is made from a kit that includes a jig with molds over which the strakes are laid.

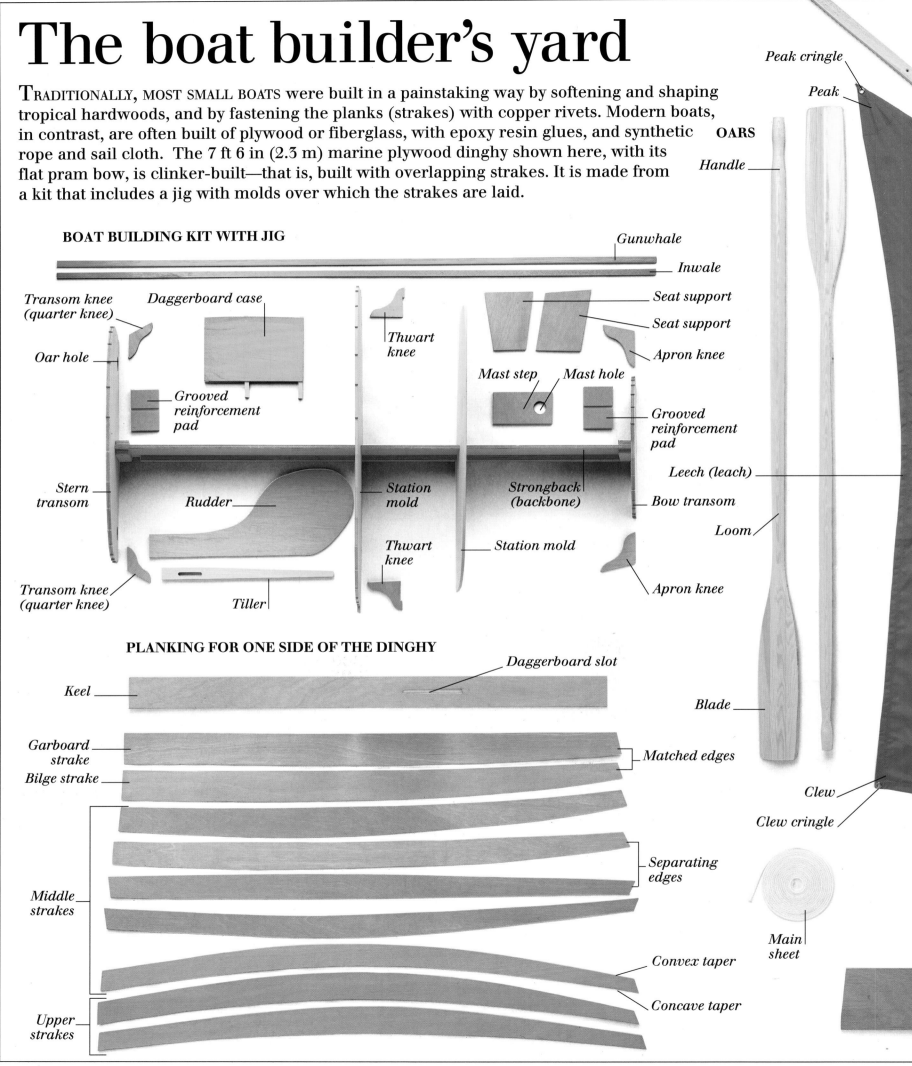

BOAT BUILDING KIT WITH JIG

Gunwhale

Inwale

Transom knee (quarter knee)

Daggerboard case

Thwart knee

Seat support

Seat support

Oar hole

Apron knee

Mast step   Mast hole

Grooved reinforcement pad

Grooved reinforcement pad

Stern transom

Rudder

Station mold

Strongback (backbone)

Bow transom

Thwart knee

Station mold

Transom knee (quarter knee)

Tiller

Apron knee

OARS

Peak cringle

Peak

Handle

Leech (leach)

Loom

PLANKING FOR ONE SIDE OF THE DINGHY

Keel

Daggerboard slot

Garboard strake

Bilge strake

Matched edges

Middle strakes

Separating edges

Blade

Clew

Clew cringle

Convex taper

Concave taper

Upper strakes

Main sheet

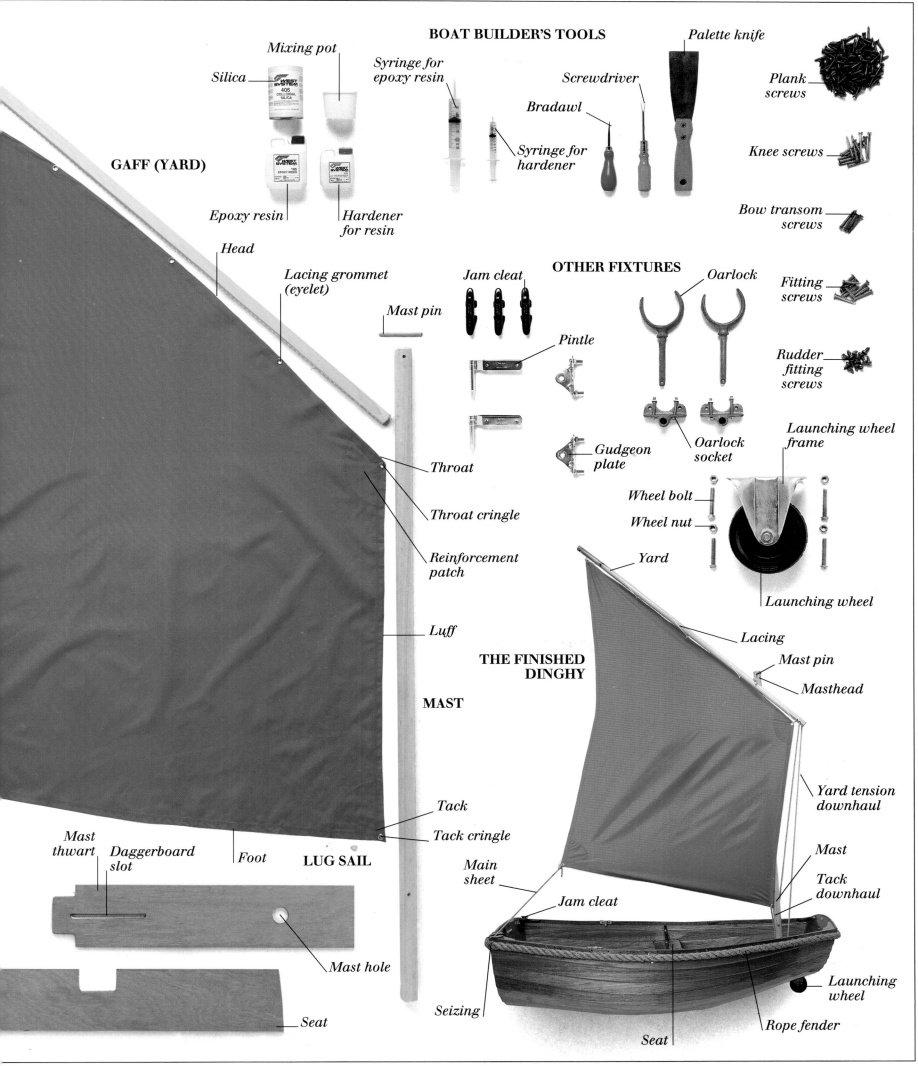

BOAT BUILDER'S TOOLS

Mixing pot

Silica

Syringe for epoxy resin

Screwdriver

Palette knife

Bradawl

Plank screws

Syringe for hardener

Knee screws

GAFF (YARD)

Epoxy resin

Hardener for resin

Bow transom screws

Head

Lacing grommet (eyelet)

OTHER FIXTURES

Jam cleat

Oarlock

Fitting screws

Mast pin

Pintle

Rudder fitting screws

Throat

Throat cringle

Gudgeon plate

Oarlock socket

Launching wheel frame

Reinforcement patch

Wheel bolt

Wheel nut

Luff

Yard

Launching wheel

THE FINISHED DINGHY

Lacing

Mast pin

Masthead

MAST

Yard tension downhaul

Tack

Tack cringle

Mast

Main sheet

Tack downhaul

Mast thwart

Daggerboard slot

Foot

LUG SAIL

Jam cleat

Mast hole

Launching wheel

Seizing

Rope fender

Seat

Seat

25

Rigging

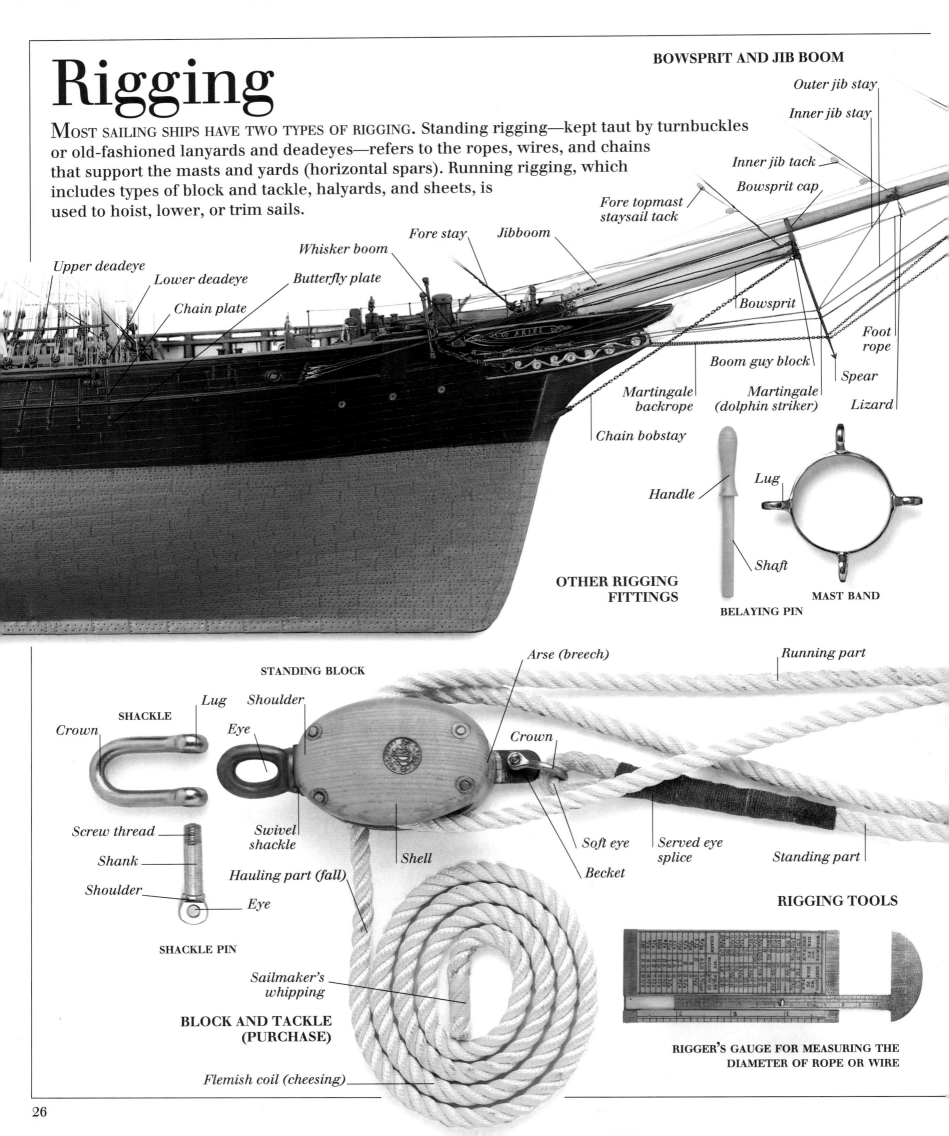

MOST SAILING SHIPS HAVE TWO TYPES OF RIGGING. Standing rigging—kept taut by turnbuckles or old-fashioned lanyards and deadeyes—refers to the ropes, wires, and chains that support the masts and yards (horizontal spars). Running rigging, which includes types of block and tackle, halyards, and sheets, is used to hoist, lower, or trim sails.

BOWSPRIT AND JIB BOOM

Outer jib stay

Inner jib stay

Inner jib tack

Bowsprit cap

Fore topmast staysail tack

Fore stay

Whisker boom

Jibboom

Upper deadeye

Lower deadeye

Butterfly plate

Chain plate

Bowsprit

Foot rope

Boom guy block

Spear

Martingale backrope

Martingale (dolphin striker)

Lizard

Chain bobstay

OTHER RIGGING FITTINGS

Handle

Lug

Shaft

BELAYING PIN

MAST BAND

Arse (breech)

Running part

STANDING BLOCK

Lug

Shoulder

SHACKLE

Eye

Crown

Crown

Screw thread

Swivel shackle

Shank

Shell

Soft eye

Served eye splice

Standing part

Shoulder

Becket

Eye

Hauling part (fall)

SHACKLE PIN

RIGGING TOOLS

Sailmaker's whipping

BLOCK AND TACKLE (PURCHASE)

Flemish coil (cheesing)

RIGGER'S GAUGE FOR MEASURING THE DIAMETER OF ROPE OR WIRE

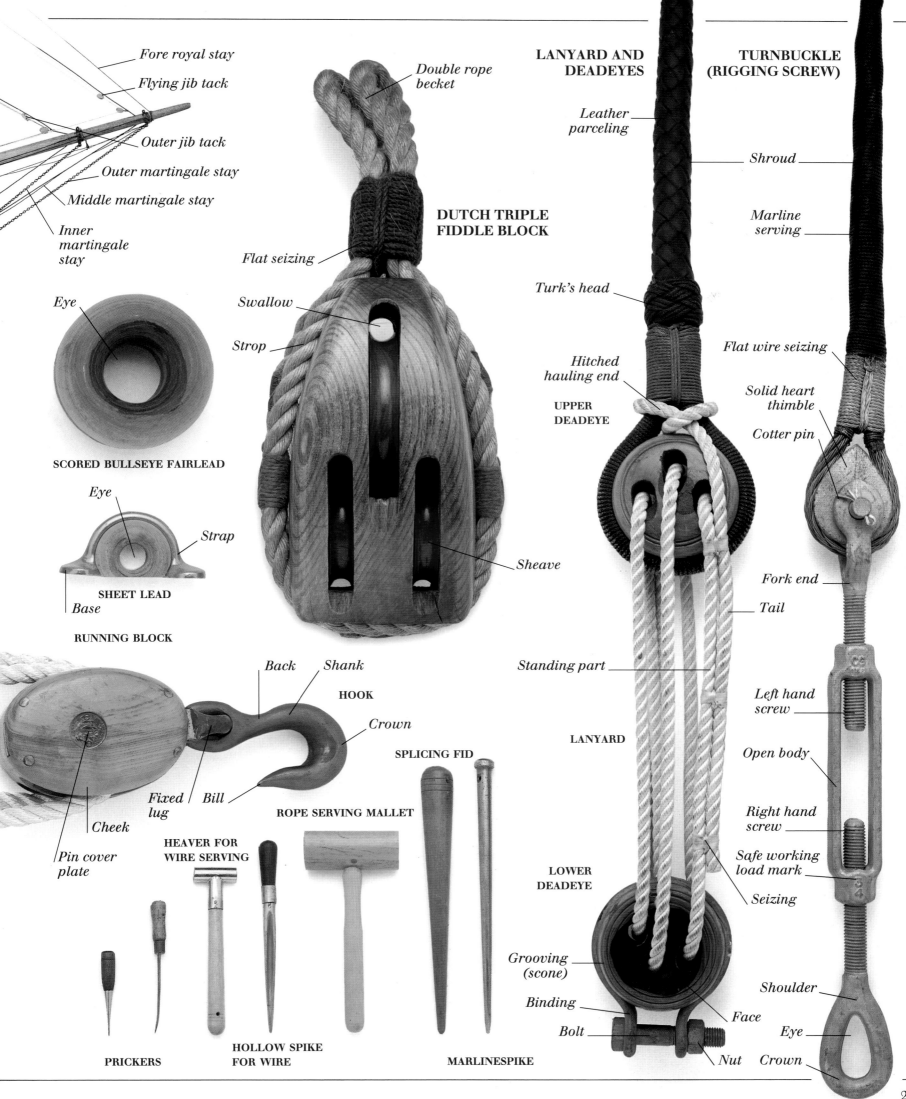

Fore royal stay

Flying jib tack

Outer jib tack

Outer martingale stay

Middle martingale stay

Inner martingale stay

Eye

SCORED BULLSEYE FAIRLEAD

Eye

Strap

SHEET LEAD

Base

RUNNING BLOCK

Double rope becket

DUTCH TRIPLE FIDDLE BLOCK

Flat seizing

Swallow

Strop

Sheave

Back   Shank

HOOK

Crown

Fixed lug   Bill

SPLICING FID

ROPE SERVING MALLET

Cheek

Pin cover plate

HEAVER FOR WIRE SERVING

HOLLOW SPIKE FOR WIRE

MARLINESPIKE

PRICKERS

LANYARD AND DEADEYES

TURNBUCKLE (RIGGING SCREW)

Leather parceling

Shroud

Marline serving

Turk's head

Hitched hauling end

UPPER DEADEYE

Flat wire seizing

Solid heart thimble

Cotter pin

Standing part

Fork end

Tail

LANYARD

Left hand screw

Open body

Right hand screw

Safe working load mark

Seizing

LOWER DEADEYE

Grooving (scone)

Binding

Bolt

Face

Nut

Shoulder

Eye

Crown

Sails

THERE ARE TWO MAIN TYPES OF SAILS: Old-fashioned square sails hang from yards at right angles
to the mast, and are powerful drivers with following winds; fore-and aft sails are set parallel to the
length of the boat, with the luff (leading edge) of the sail attached to a mast or a stay. They are
more efficient for all-round sailing, and almost all modern sailboats are rigged this way. Some
fore-and-aft sails have a gaff at the head; Marconi-rig sails are pointed at the top (below). The bottom (foot)
of the sail is on a boom. Sails are made of strips of cloth sewn together. Cotton and flax are traditional sail
materials but synthetic fabrics are now more often used.

TOP OF A MARCONI SAIL

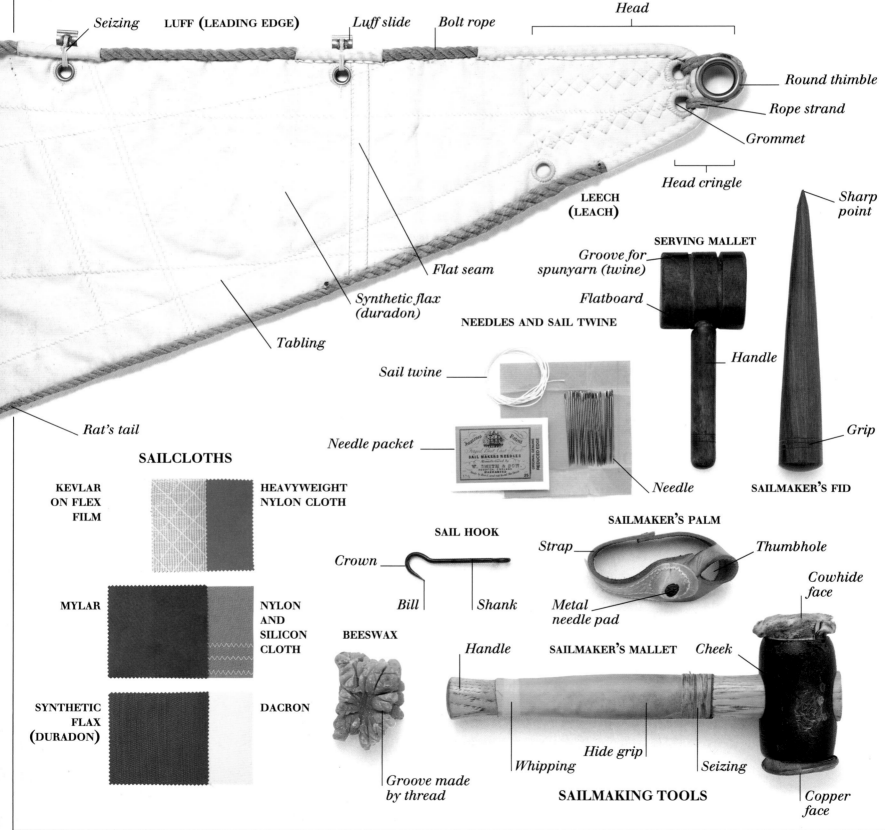

Seizing   LUFF (LEADING EDGE)   Luff slide   Bolt rope   Head

Round thimble

Rope strand

Grommet

Head cringle

LEECH
(LEACH)

Sharp
point

Flat seam

SERVING MALLET

Groove for
spunyarn (twine)

Synthetic flax
(duradon)

Flatboard

Handle

NEEDLES AND SAIL TWINE

Tabling

Sail twine

Rat's tail

Needle packet

Grip

SAILCLOTHS

Needle

SAILMAKER'S FID

KEVLAR
ON FLEX
FILM

HEAVYWEIGHT
NYLON CLOTH

SAIL HOOK

SAILMAKER'S PALM

Strap

Thumbhole

Crown

Cowhide
face

MYLAR

NYLON
AND
SILICON
CLOTH

Bill   Shank

Metal
needle pad

BEESWAX

Handle

SAILMAKER'S MALLET

Cheek

SYNTHETIC
FLAX
(DURADON)

DACRON

Groove made
by thread

Whipping

Hide grip

Seizing

SAILMAKING TOOLS

Copper
face

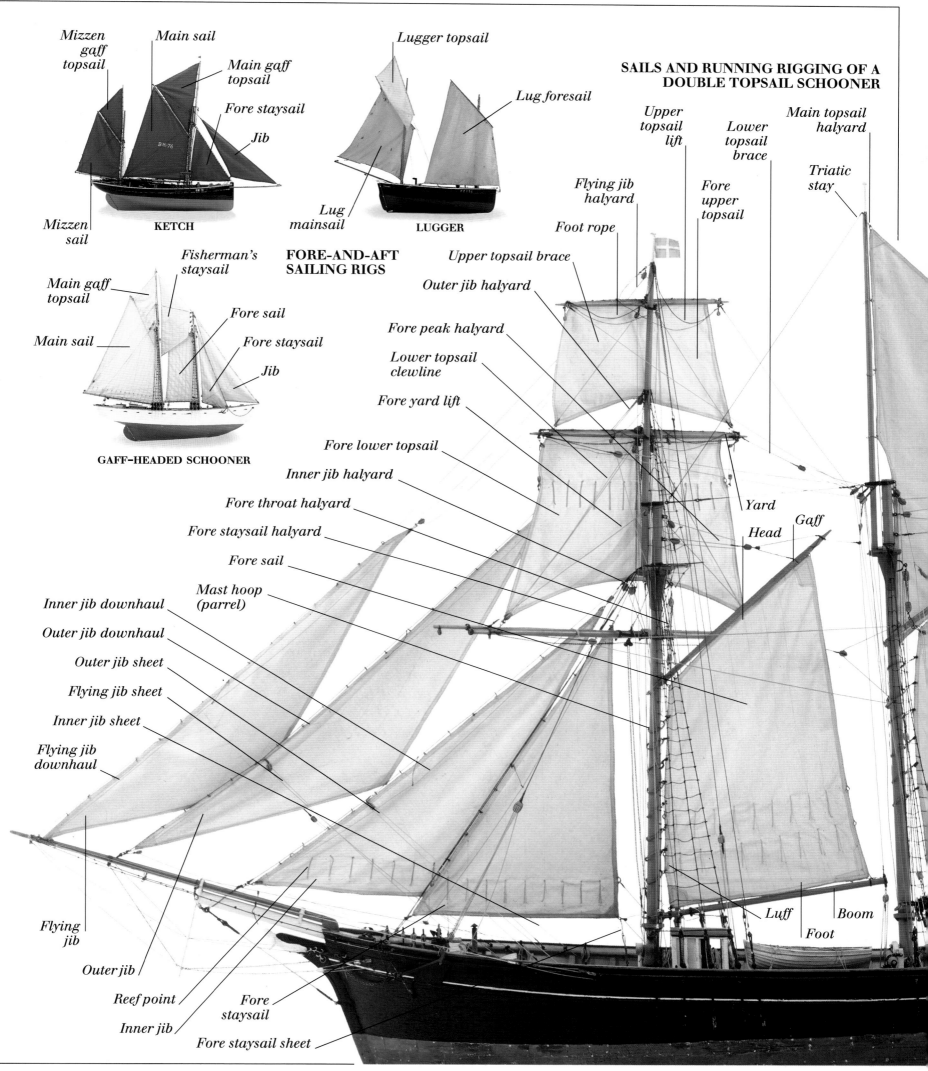

Mizzen gaff topsail

Main sail

Main gaff topsail

Fore staysail

Jib

Mizzen sail

KETCH

Lugger topsail

Lug foresail

Lug mainsail

LUGGER

SAILS AND RUNNING RIGGING OF A DOUBLE TOPSAIL SCHOONER

Upper topsail lift

Lower topsail brace

Main topsail halyard

Flying jib halyard

Fore upper topsail

Triatic stay

Foot rope

Upper topsail brace

Outer jib halyard

Fisherman's staysail

Main gaff topsail

Fore sail

Main sail

Fore staysail

Jib

Fore peak halyard

Lower topsail clewline

FORE-AND-AFT SAILING RIGS

GAFF-HEADED SCHOONER

Fore yard lift

Fore lower topsail

Inner jib halyard

Fore throat halyard

Fore staysail halyard

Fore sail

Mast hoop (parrel)

Inner jib downhaul

Outer jib downhaul

Outer jib sheet

Flying jib sheet

Inner jib sheet

Flying jib downhaul

Yard

Head

Gaff

Luff

Boom

Foot

Flying jib

Outer jib

Reef point

Fore staysail

Inner jib

Fore staysail sheet

29

Man-powered craft

WHILE MANY MAN-POWERED CRAFT HAVE CHANGED LITTLE since the first boats, others have been developed for specific purposes, such as hauling goods, fishing, and sport. The cargo-carrying Bangladeshi dinghy is paddled or punted with a pole. The early Britons' coracle is still used for fishing. It is paddled over the bow with one hand only, while the other hand tends the fishing net. Most rowboats are rowed, or sculled, with a pair of oars worked in a continuous cycle of strokes. ("Sculling" can also mean to use just one oar over the stern of a small boat.) The scull shown at bottom is a super-light, fast sport craft with a sliding seat whose oars pivot on riggers to give more leverage. The canoe opposite has an outrigger to keep it from turning over.

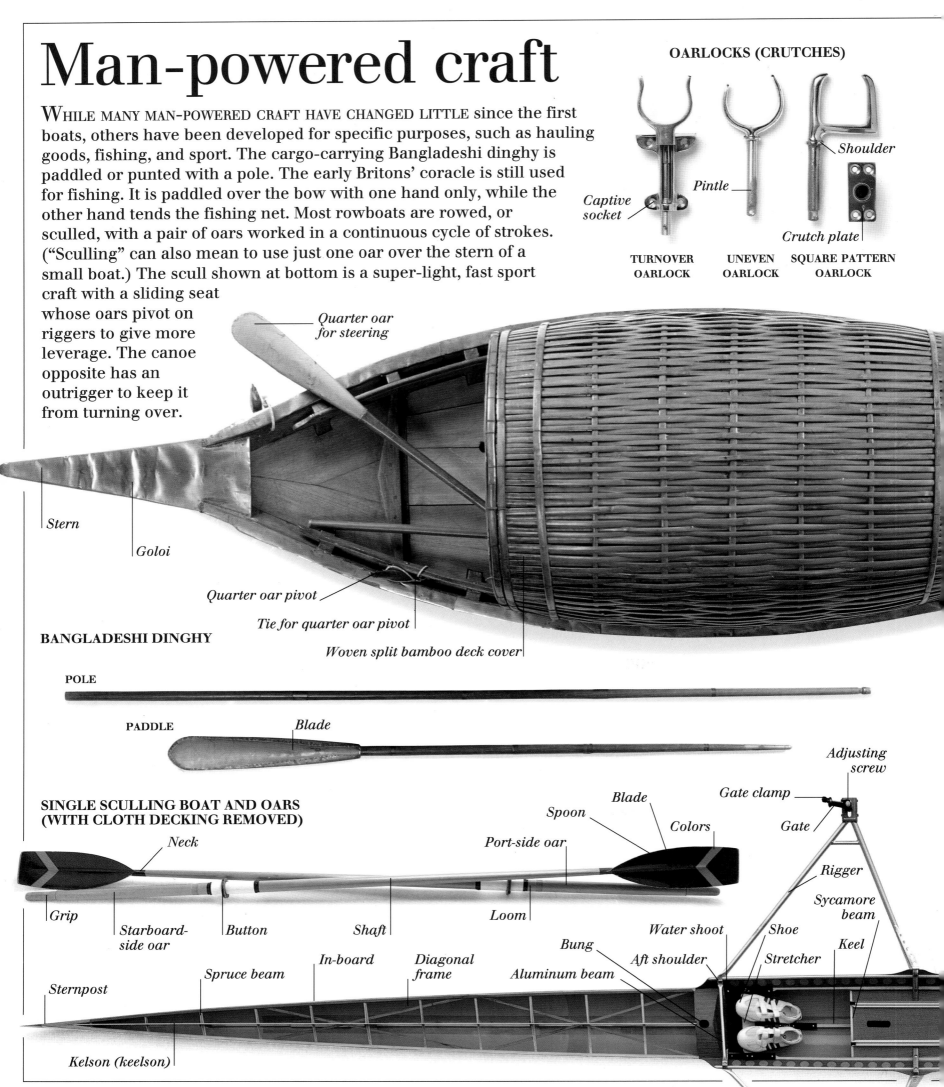

OARLOCKS (CRUTCHES)

Shoulder

Pintle

Captive socket

Crutch plate

TURNOVER OARLOCK   UNEVEN OARLOCK   SQUARE PATTERN OARLOCK

Quarter oar for steering

Stern

Goloi

Quarter oar pivot

Tie for quarter oar pivot

Woven split bamboo deck cover

BANGLADESHI DINGHY

POLE

PADDLE   Blade

SINGLE SCULLING BOAT AND OARS (WITH CLOTH DECKING REMOVED)

Neck

Spoon

Blade

Colors

Port-side oar

Adjusting screw

Gate clamp

Gate

Rigger

Sycamore beam

Grip

Starboard-side oar

Button

Shaft

Loom

Water shoot

Shoe

Keel

Sternpost

Spruce beam

In-board

Diagonal frame

Bung

Aft shoulder

Stretcher

Aluminum beam

Kelson (keelson)

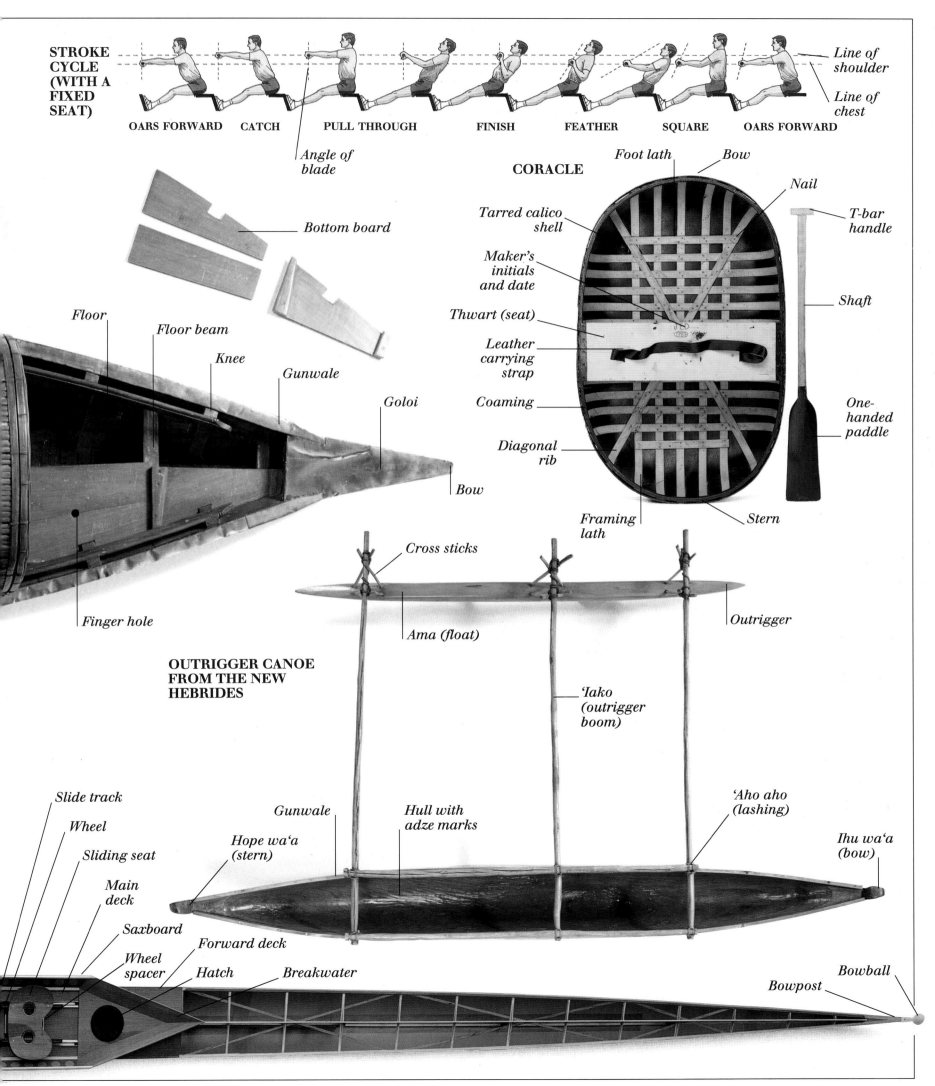

STROKE CYCLE (WITH A FIXED SEAT)

Line of shoulder

Line of chest

OARS FORWARD CATCH PULL THROUGH FINISH FEATHER SQUARE OARS FORWARD

Angle of blade

Bottom board

CORACLE

Foot lath

Bow

Nail

T-bar handle

Tarred calico shell

Shaft

Maker's initials and date

Thwart (seat)

Leather carrying strap

One-handed paddle

Coaming

Diagonal rib

Framing lath

Stern

Floor

Floor beam

Knee

Gunwale

Goloi

Bow

Finger hole

Cross sticks

Ama (float)

Outrigger

OUTRIGGER CANOE FROM THE NEW HEBRIDES

'Iako (outrigger boom)

Slide track

Wheel

Sliding seat

Main deck

Saxboard

Wheel spacer

Forward deck

Hatch

Breakwater

Gunwale

Hope wa'a (stern)

Hull with adze marks

'Aho aho (lashing)

Ihu wa'a (bow)

Bowball

Bowpost

31

Directions

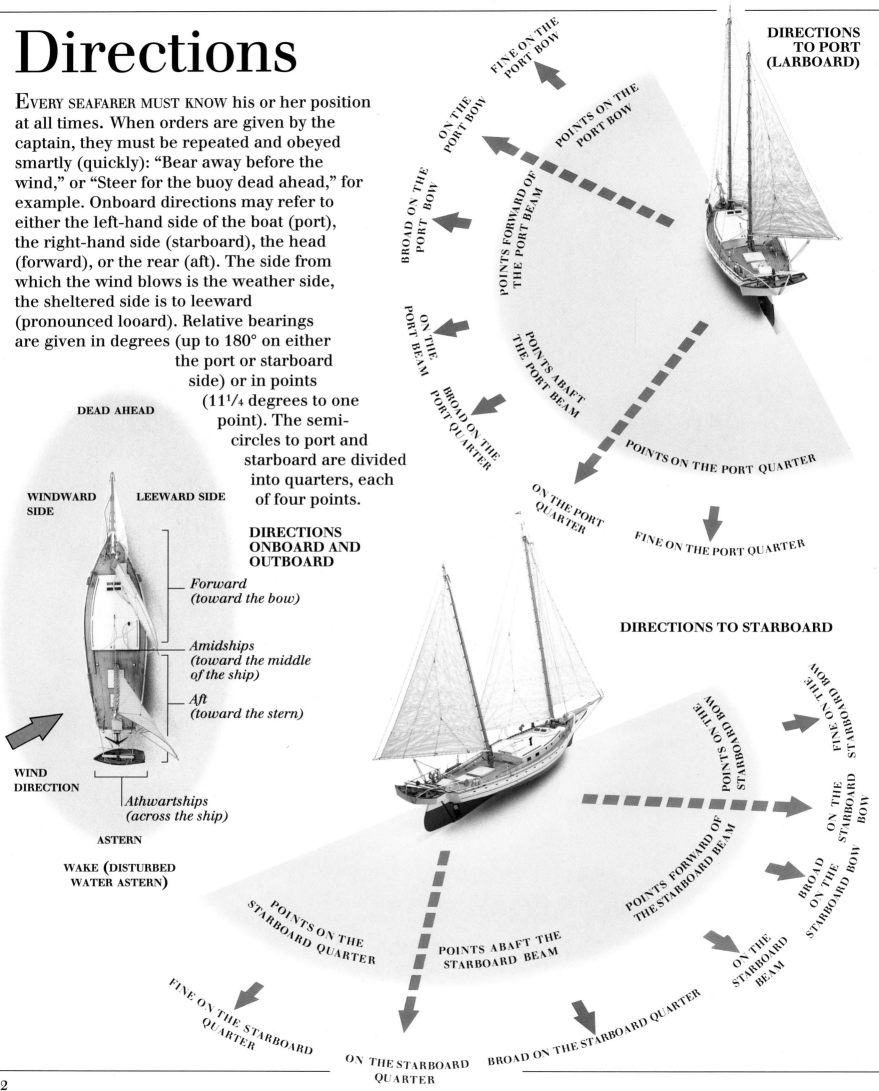

EVERY SEAFARER MUST KNOW his or her position at all times. When orders are given by the captain, they must be repeated and obeyed smartly (quickly): "Bear away before the wind," or "Steer for the buoy dead ahead," for example. Onboard directions may refer to either the left-hand side of the boat (port), the right-hand side (starboard), the head (forward), or the rear (aft). The side from which the wind blows is the weather side, the sheltered side is to leeward (pronounced looard). Relative bearings are given in degrees (up to 180° on either the port or starboard side) or in points (11¼ degrees to one point). The semi-circles to port and starboard are divided into quarters, each of four points.

DEAD AHEAD

WINDWARD SIDE

LEEWARD SIDE

DIRECTIONS ONBOARD AND OUTBOARD

Forward (toward the bow)

Amidships (toward the middle of the ship)

Aft (toward the stern)

WIND DIRECTION

Athwartships (across the ship)

ASTERN

WAKE (DISTURBED WATER ASTERN)

DIRECTIONS TO PORT (LARBOARD)

FINE ON THE PORT BOW

POINTS ON THE PORT BOW

ON THE PORT BOW

BROAD ON THE PORT BOW

POINTS FORWARD OF THE PORT BEAM

ON THE PORT BEAM

POINTS ABAFT THE PORT BEAM

BROAD ON THE PORT QUARTER

POINTS ON THE PORT QUARTER

ON THE PORT QUARTER

FINE ON THE PORT QUARTER

DIRECTIONS TO STARBOARD

FINE ON THE STARBOARD BOW

POINTS ON THE STARBOARD BOW

ON THE STARBOARD BOW

BROAD ON THE STARBOARD BOW

POINTS FORWARD OF THE STARBOARD BEAM

ON THE STARBOARD BEAM

POINTS ABAFT THE STARBOARD BEAM

BROAD ON THE STARBOARD QUARTER

POINTS ON THE STARBOARD QUARTER

ON THE STARBOARD QUARTER

FINE ON THE STARBOARD QUARTER

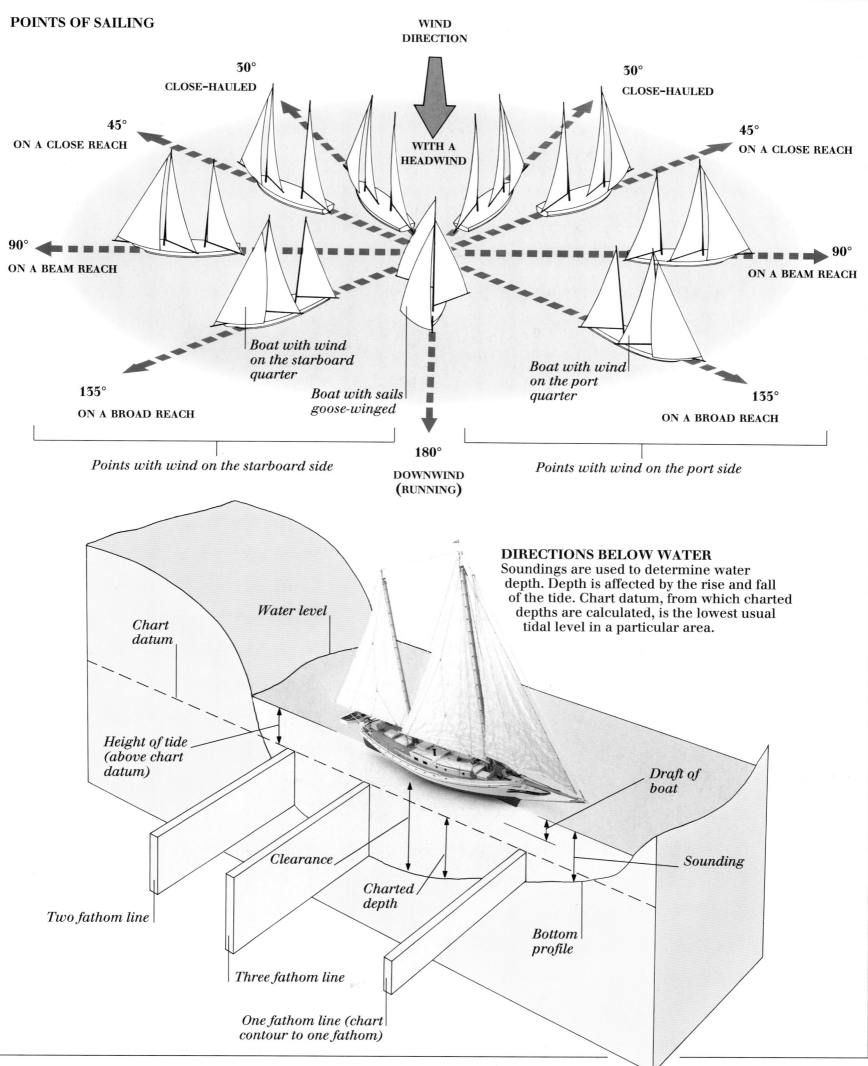

POINTS OF SAILING

WIND DIRECTION

30°
CLOSE-HAULED

30°
CLOSE-HAULED

45°
ON A CLOSE REACH

45°
ON A CLOSE REACH

WITH A HEADWIND

90°
ON A BEAM REACH

90°
ON A BEAM REACH

Boat with wind on the starboard quarter

Boat with wind on the port quarter

Boat with sails goose-winged

135°
ON A BROAD REACH

135°
ON A BROAD REACH

Points with wind on the starboard side

Points with wind on the port side

180°
DOWNWIND (RUNNING)

DIRECTIONS BELOW WATER

Soundings are used to determine water depth. Depth is affected by the rise and fall of the tide. Chart datum, from which charted depths are calculated, is the lowest usual tidal level in a particular area.

Chart datum

Water level

Height of tide (above chart datum)

Draft of boat

Clearance

Sounding

Two fathom line

Charted depth

Bottom profile

Three fathom line

One fathom line (chart contour to one fathom)

Navigation

NAVIGATION IS THE ART OF GUIDING A SHIP SAFELY between two points defined in terms of their latitude and longitude. Sailors in early times relied on landmarks for direction, while the watchkeeper turned an hourglass to indicate how long the ship had been following a given compass course. Like the cross-stave and the astrolabe, the sextant enabled sailors to measure their latitude by showing the angle between two known objects or between a heavenly body and the horizon. The chronometer allowed the mariner to calculate longitude accurately, by comparing local time with a fixed time standard. Speed and distance run were found at sea by trailing astern a taffrail log, as shown opposite.

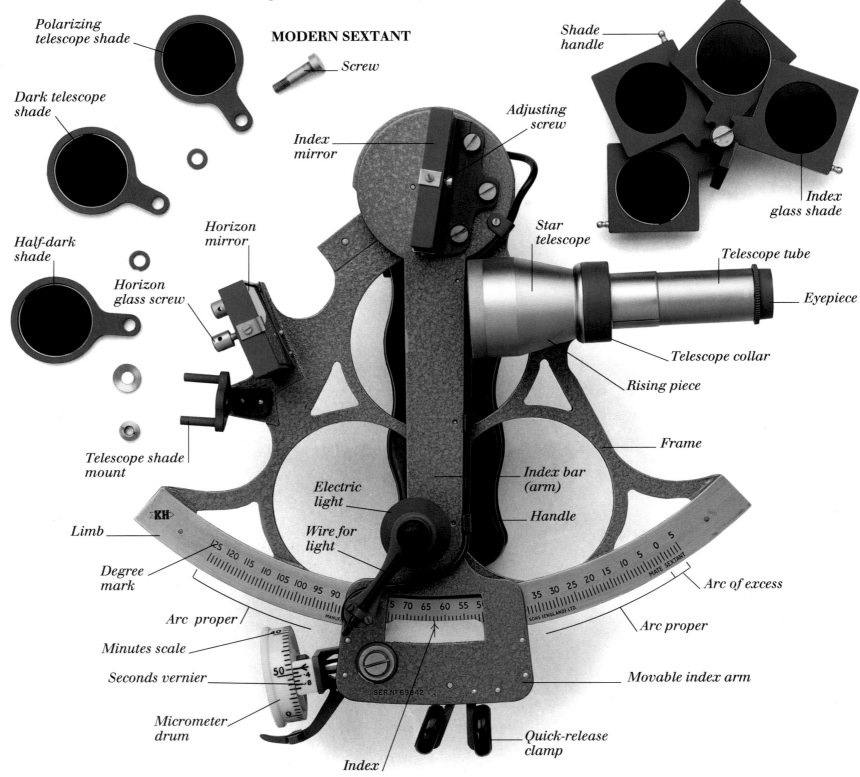

Telescope

Limb

EARLY SEXTANT

Polarizing telescope shade

Dark telescope shade

Half-dark shade

MODERN SEXTANT

Screw

Horizon mirror

Horizon glass screw

Telescope shade mount

Index mirror

Adjusting screw

Star telescope

Electric light

Index bar (arm)

Handle

Wire for light

Shade handle

Index glass shade

Telescope tube

Eyepiece

Telescope collar

Rising piece

Frame

Limb

Degree mark

Arc proper

Minutes scale

Seconds vernier

Micrometer drum

Index

Arc of excess

Arc proper

Movable index arm

Quick-release clamp

125 120 115 110 105 100 95 90

5 70 65 60 55 5

35 30 25 20 15 10 5 5

KH

MATE SEXTANT

SONS (ENGLAND) LTD.

SER. N° 69842

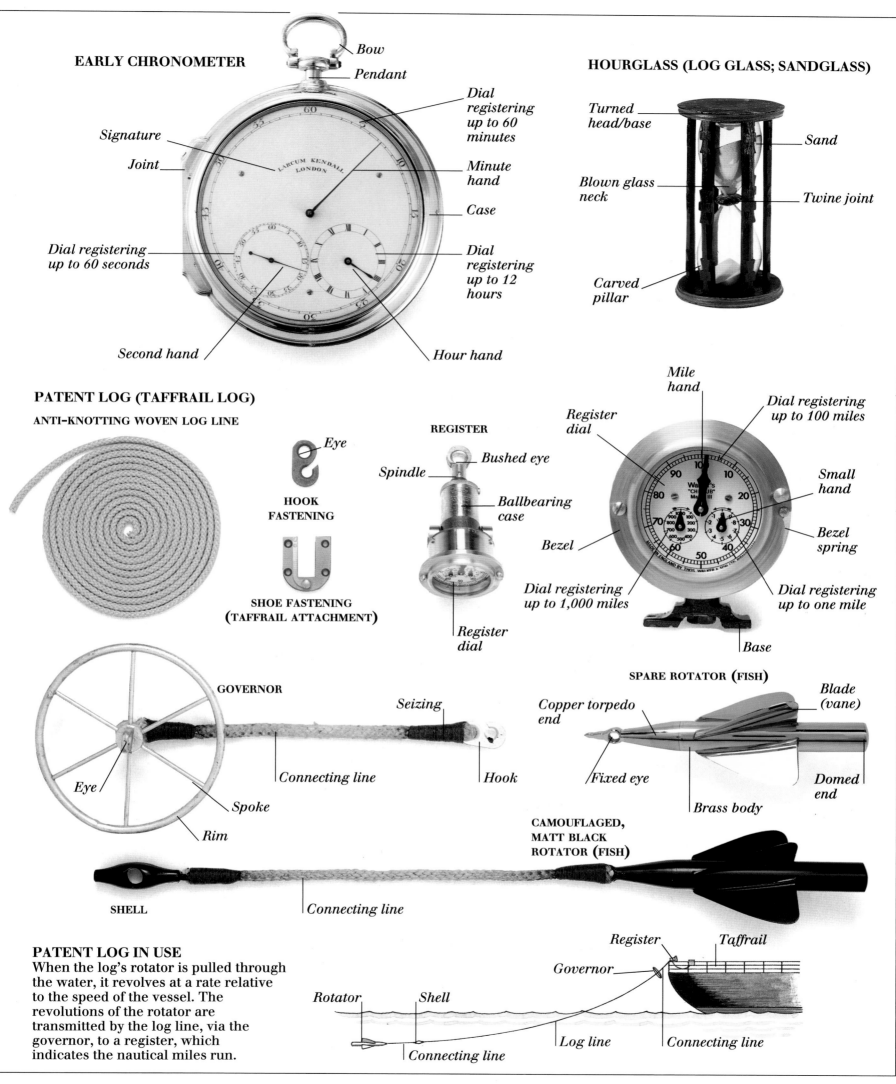

EARLY CHRONOMETER

Bow

Pendant

Dial registering up to 60 minutes

Signature

Joint

LARCUM KENDALL LONDON

Minute hand

Case

Dial registering up to 60 seconds

Dial registering up to 12 hours

Second hand

Hour hand

HOURGLASS (LOG GLASS; SANDGLASS)

Turned head/base

Sand

Blown glass neck

Twine joint

Carved pillar

PATENT LOG (TAFFRAIL LOG)

ANTI-KNOTTING WOVEN LOG LINE

Eye

HOOK FASTENING

SHOE FASTENING (TAFFRAIL ATTACHMENT)

REGISTER

Spindle

Bushed eye

Ballbearing case

Register dial

Register dial

Mile hand

Dial registering up to 100 miles

Register dial

Small hand

Walker's "CHERUB" Mark III

Bezel

Bezel spring

MADE IN ENGLAND BY THOS. WALKER & SON, TYSELEY

Dial registering up to 1,000 miles

Dial registering up to one mile

Base

GOVERNOR

Seizing

Connecting line

Hook

Eye

Spoke

Rim

SPARE ROTATOR (FISH)

Copper torpedo end

Blade (vane)

Fixed eye

Brass body

Domed end

CAMOUFLAGED, MATT BLACK ROTATOR (FISH)

SHELL

Connecting line

PATENT LOG IN USE

When the log's rotator is pulled through the water, it revolves at a rate relative to the speed of the vessel. The revolutions of the rotator are transmitted by the log line, via the governor, to a register, which indicates the nautical miles run.

Register

Taffrail

Governor

Rotator

Shell

Log line

Connecting line

Connecting line

Piloting

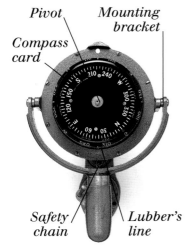

Pivot
Mounting bracket
Compass card
Safety chain
Lubber's line

MAGNETIC COMPASS

Navigating a ship in waters where charted landmarks, lighthouses, or buoys are visible is the art of piloting. Mariners have many aids to help them find their way when piloting. The magnetic compass is based on the attraction of a magnet to magnetic north. A round compass card rests on a pivot, held steady by magnetism; it is marked with 360° or a series of directional "points." These indicate the ship's course. The compass is often housed in a binnacle, a wooden case with correctors that counter the magnetic distortion of an iron ship. Most vessels now use electronic devices to find water depth, but some still use the lead line, marked in fathoms. (A fathom is six feet.) Terms such as "and a half one" indicate fractions of a fathom. Lighthouses flash lights in regular sequences that are marked on nautical charts. Buoys are floating marks that warn of dangers or show safe channels. Shape, color, and sometimes "top-marks" distinguish one buoy from another. Those shown opposite are commonly found in European waters.

BINNACLE

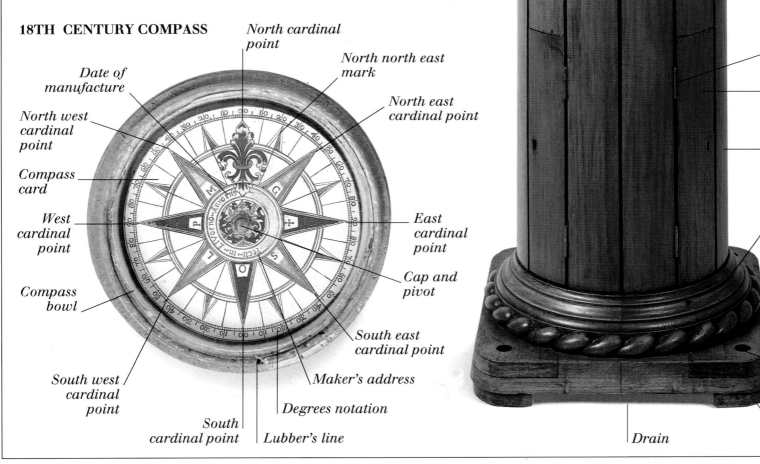

18TH CENTURY COMPASS

North cardinal point
North north east mark
North east cardinal point
Date of manufacture
North west cardinal point
Compass card
West cardinal point
East cardinal point
Compass bowl
Cap and pivot
South east cardinal point
South west cardinal point
Maker's address
Degrees notation
South cardinal point
Lubber's line

Hood (cowl)
Shutter covering compass card
Lamp receptacle
Clinometer
Soft iron sphere (quadrantal corrector)
Grooved bracket for sphere
Maker's nameplate
Door to corrector magnets
Hinge
Rebated panel
Wooden case
Circular molding
Wooden rope molding
Base
Bolt hole
Corner pad
Drain

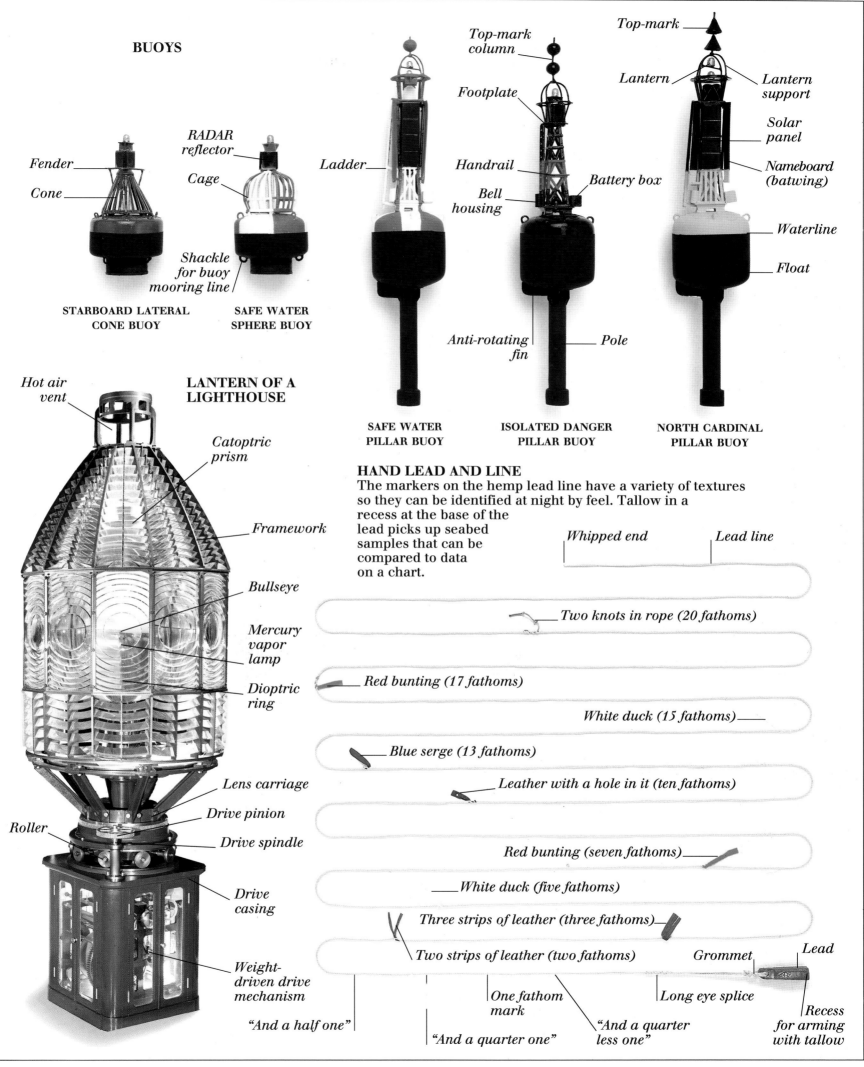

BUOYS

STARBOARD LATERAL CONE BUOY
- Fender
- Cone

SAFE WATER SPHERE BUOY
- RADAR reflector
- Cage
- Shackle for buoy mooring line

SAFE WATER PILLAR BUOY
- Ladder
- Top-mark column

ISOLATED DANGER PILLAR BUOY
- Footplate
- Handrail
- Bell housing
- Battery box
- Anti-rotating fin
- Pole

NORTH CARDINAL PILLAR BUOY
- Top-mark
- Lantern
- Lantern support
- Solar panel
- Nameboard (batwing)
- Waterline
- Float

LANTERN OF A LIGHTHOUSE
- Hot air vent
- Catoptric prism
- Framework
- Bullseye
- Mercury vapor lamp
- Dioptric ring
- Lens carriage
- Drive pinion
- Drive spindle
- Roller
- Drive casing
- Weight-driven drive mechanism

HAND LEAD AND LINE

The markers on the hemp lead line have a variety of textures so they can be identified at night by feel. Tallow in a recess at the base of the lead picks up seabed samples that can be compared to data on a chart.

- Whipped end
- Lead line
- Two knots in rope (20 fathoms)
- Red bunting (17 fathoms)
- White duck (15 fathoms)
- Blue serge (13 fathoms)
- Leather with a hole in it (ten fathoms)
- Red bunting (seven fathoms)
- White duck (five fathoms)
- Three strips of leather (three fathoms)
- Two strips of leather (two fathoms)
- Grommet
- Lead
- One fathom mark
- Long eye splice
- Recess for arming with tallow
- "And a half one"
- "And a quarter one"
- "And a quarter less one"

Charts and piloting tools

EARLY SEAFARERS COULD CALCULATE THEIR LATITUDE by observing the altitude of certain stars identified from a celestial globe. Modern charts show lines of latitude (parallels)—measured in degrees, minutes, and seconds north or south of the equator—and lines of longitude (meridians)—measured east or west from zero longitude at Greenwich, England. A rhumb line intersects all meridians at the same angle; to follow a rhumb line ensures that the navigator keeps a constant course. The chart also shows sea depths, coastlines, shore elevations, lights, buoys, and other features identifiable from a ship. Parallel rulers and the plotter are used in working out courses on a chart, while dividers help measure the distance between charted points. The hand-bearing compass has a sight that a navigator lines up with visible objects, so as to obtain their compass bearings. True north is at the North Pole; note that magnetic north (to which a compass needle points) is actually in the middle of the Canadian Arctic.

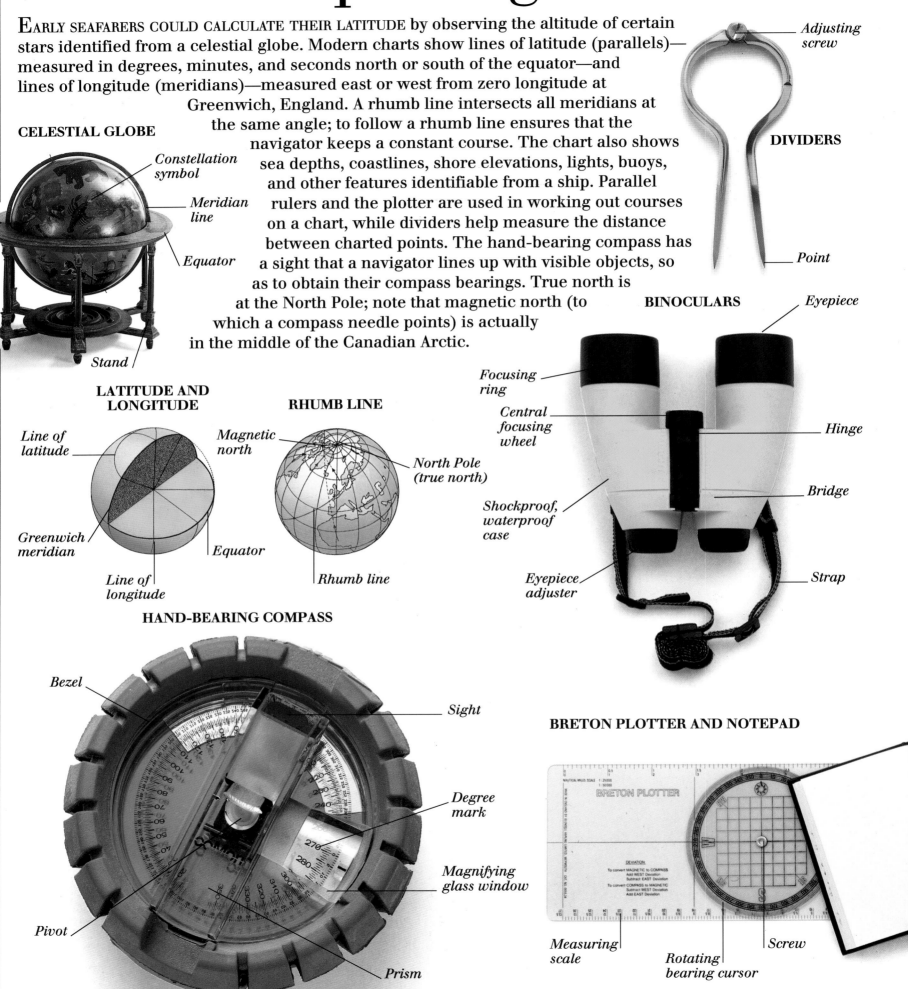

DIVIDERS

Adjusting screw

Point

CELESTIAL GLOBE

Constellation symbol

Meridian line

Equator

Stand

LATITUDE AND LONGITUDE

Line of latitude

Greenwich meridian

Line of longitude

Equator

RHUMB LINE

Magnetic north

North Pole (true north)

Rhumb line

BINOCULARS

Eyepiece

Focusing ring

Central focusing wheel

Hinge

Shockproof, waterproof case

Bridge

Eyepiece adjuster

Strap

HAND-BEARING COMPASS

Bezel

Sight

Degree mark

Magnifying glass window

Pivot

Prism

BRETON PLOTTER AND NOTEPAD

NAUTICAL MILES SCALE 1 : 25000
1 : 50000

BRETON PLOTTER

DEVIATION

To convert MAGNETIC to COMPASS
Add WEST Deviation
Subtract EAST Deviation

To convert COMPASS to MAGNETIC
Subtract WEST Deviation
Add EAST Deviation

Measuring scale

Rotating bearing cursor

Screw

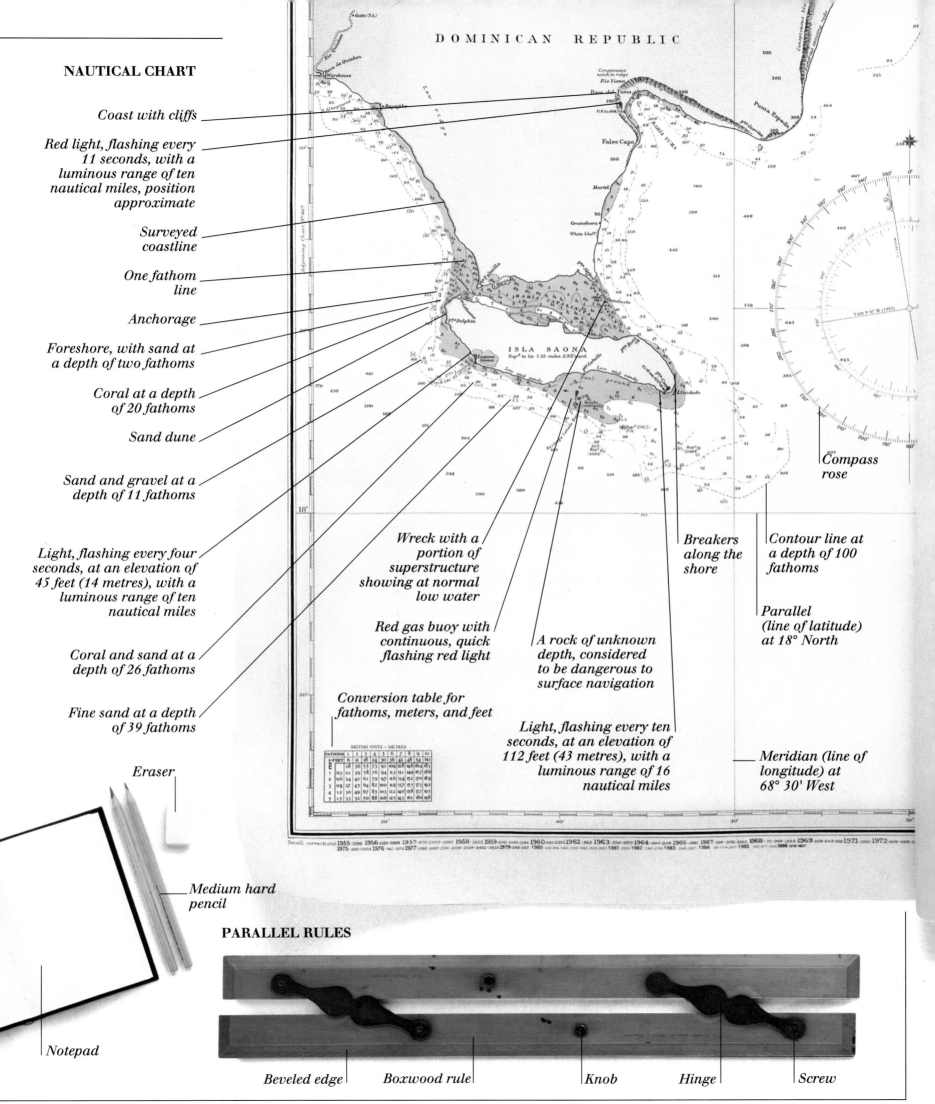

NAUTICAL CHART

- Coast with cliffs
- Red light, flashing every 11 seconds, with a luminous range of ten nautical miles, position approximate
- Surveyed coastline
- One fathom line
- Anchorage
- Foreshore, with sand at a depth of two fathoms
- Coral at a depth of 20 fathoms
- Sand dune
- Sand and gravel at a depth of 11 fathoms
- Light, flashing every four seconds, at an elevation of 45 feet (14 metres), with a luminous range of ten nautical miles
- Coral and sand at a depth of 26 fathoms
- Fine sand at a depth of 39 fathoms

DOMINICAN REPUBLIC

ISLA SAONA

- Wreck with a portion of superstructure showing at normal low water
- Red gas buoy with continuous, quick flashing red light
- Conversion table for fathoms, meters, and feet
- A rock of unknown depth, considered to be dangerous to surface navigation
- Light, flashing every ten seconds, at an elevation of 112 feet (43 metres), with a luminous range of 16 nautical miles
- Breakers along the shore
- Contour line at a depth of 100 fathoms
- Parallel (line of latitude) at 18° North
- Meridian (line of longitude) at 68° 30' West

Compass rose

- Eraser
- Medium hard pencil
- Notepad

PARALLEL RULES

- Beveled edge
- Boxwood rule
- Knob
- Hinge
- Screw

Flags

FOR CENTURIES, FLAGS HAVE BEEN USED TO IDENTIFY SHIPS and to pass messages from one vessel to another—either friend or foe. Each signal flag or combination of flags has a different meaning, which on sailing vessels can be changed by hoisting them on different masts. Flags are still important on ships today; national flags or ensigns identify a ship's country of origin, and standardized alphabet and number flags can be used to spell out messages. The flag of a country whose waters a ship is entering must be flown as a matter of courtesy. Solo international code flags convey specific messages, as shown on the opposite page. Other flag systems are meant for specialized jobs. For example, signalers still sometimes use semaphore code to pass messages over short distances.

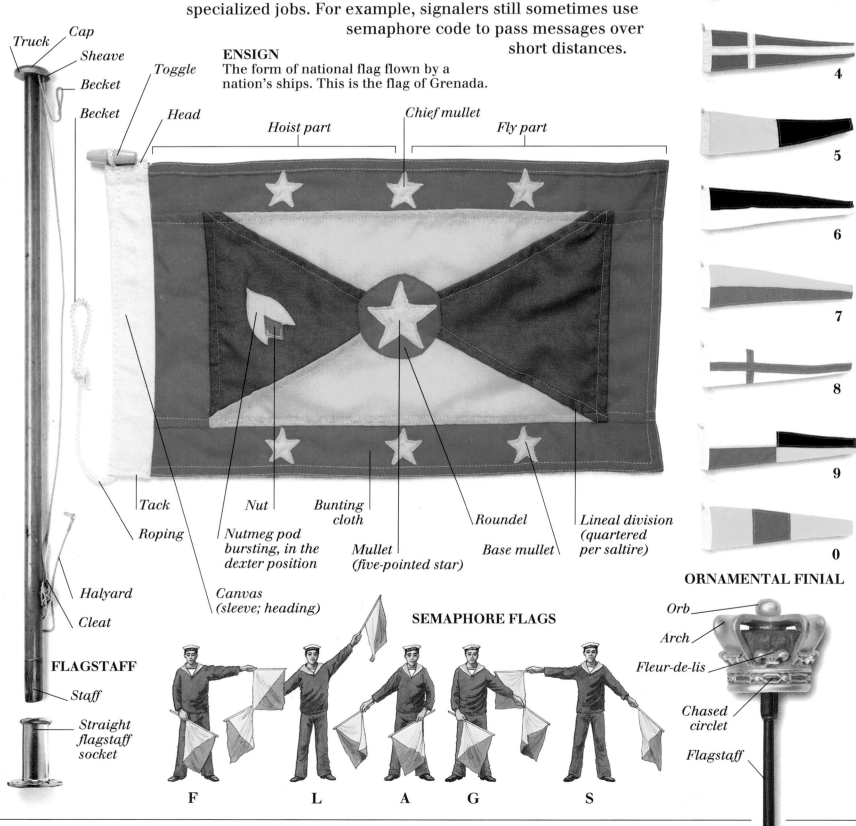

Truck
Cap
Sheave
Becket
Toggle
Becket
Head

ENSIGN
The form of national flag flown by a nation's ships. This is the flag of Grenada.

Hoist part
Chief mullet
Fly part

Tack
Nut
Bunting cloth
Roundel
Lineal division (quartered per saltire)
Roping
Nutmeg pod bursting, in the dexter position
Mullet (five-pointed star)
Base mullet
Canvas (sleeve; heading)

Halyard
Cleat

FLAGSTAFF
Staff
Straight flagstaff socket

SEMAPHORE FLAGS

F   L   A   G   S

1
2
3
4
5
6
7
8
9
0

ORNAMENTAL FINIAL
Orb
Arch
Fleur-de-lis
Chased circlet
Flagstaff

A KEEP WELL CLEAR AT LOW SPEED

B I AM CARRYING DANGEROUS GOODS

C YES (AFFIRMATIVE)

D I AM MANEUVERING WITH DIFFICULTY

E I AM DIRECTING MY COURSE TO STARBOARD

F I AM DISABLED; COMMUNICATE WITH ME

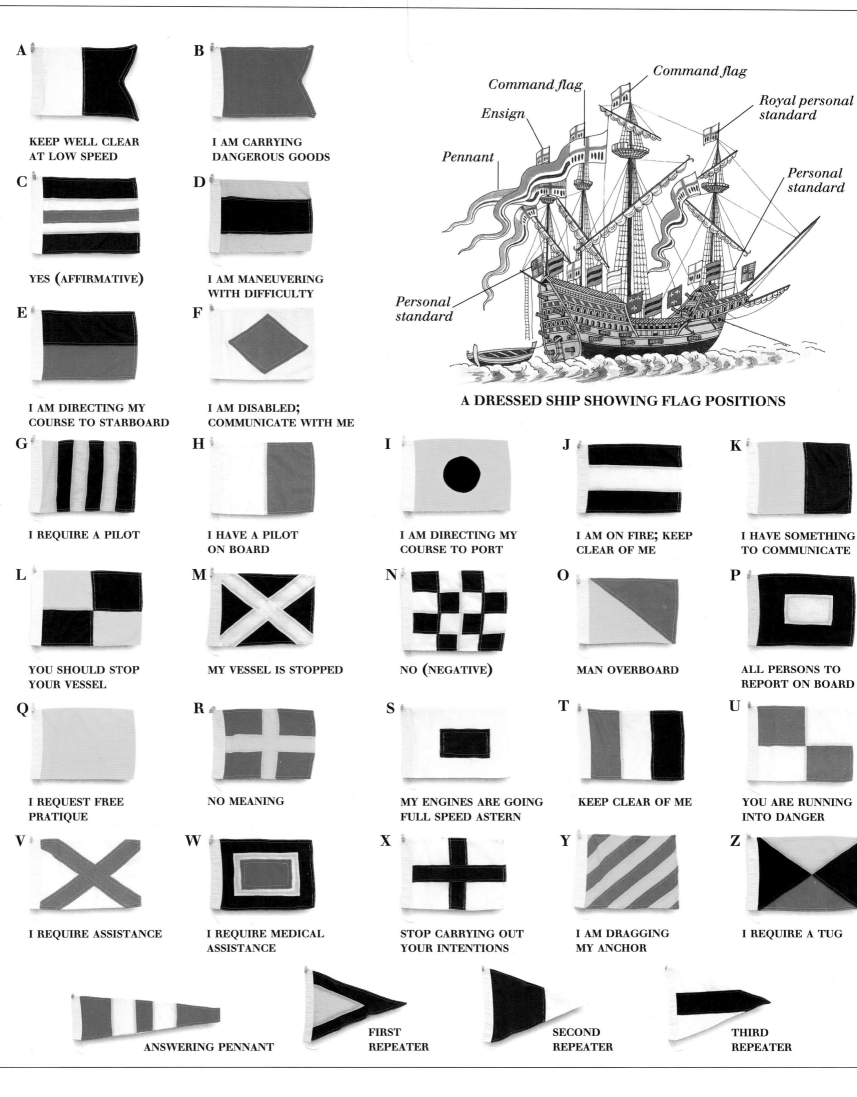

A DRESSED SHIP SHOWING FLAG POSITIONS

Command flag

Command flag

Ensign

Royal personal standard

Pennant

Personal standard

Personal standard

G I REQUIRE A PILOT

H I HAVE A PILOT ON BOARD

I I AM DIRECTING MY COURSE TO PORT

J I AM ON FIRE; KEEP CLEAR OF ME

K I HAVE SOMETHING TO COMMUNICATE

L YOU SHOULD STOP YOUR VESSEL

M MY VESSEL IS STOPPED

N NO (NEGATIVE)

O MAN OVERBOARD

P ALL PERSONS TO REPORT ON BOARD

Q I REQUEST FREE PRATIQUE

R NO MEANING

S MY ENGINES ARE GOING FULL SPEED ASTERN

T KEEP CLEAR OF ME

U YOU ARE RUNNING INTO DANGER

V I REQUIRE ASSISTANCE

W I REQUIRE MEDICAL ASSISTANCE

X STOP CARRYING OUT YOUR INTENTIONS

Y I AM DRAGGING MY ANCHOR

Z I REQUIRE A TUG

ANSWERING PENNANT

FIRST REPEATER

SECOND REPEATER

THIRD REPEATER

41

Signals

LIKE FLAGS, SOUND AND LIGHT SIGNALS are used to inform other vessels of a ship's movements. Signaling systems overlap and are complementary to one another. The Very pistol was designed to fire pyrotechnic lights of various colors and patterns that conveyed messages to other craft or to the shore. Today, the Very pistol is sometimes used to fire distress signals. Morse code is a language of dots and dashes that spells out messages when produced by sound or light. The interval of one dash is equal to three dots. The Aldis lamp sends light messages in morse code by means of a trigger-operated shutter. Calls made on a boatswain's pipe pass orders and information to a ship's crew. Navigation lights, or running lights, identify the port and starboard sides of a ship at night. In poor visibility, the fog horn must be sounded; combinations of short and long blasts convey particular meanings. When helping another ship to moor or come alongside, sailors use a code of hand signals, shown opposite. The ship's bell is used primarily to signal the time.

Crown

Wire

Engraved lettering

MAURETANIA

Shoulder

Waist

Wire

Lip

Mouth

SHIP'S BELL
Throughout each four-hour watch, hours and half-hours are struck by a ship's bell. The time is described as "one bell" for the first half hour, "two bells" for the second half hour, and so on, up to eight bells.

Muzzle

Barrel

MORSE CODE

A • ▬	J • ▬ ▬ ▬	R • ▬ •
B ▬ • • •	K ▬ • ▬	S • • •
C ▬ • ▬ •	L • ▬ • •	T ▬
D ▬ • •	M ▬ ▬	U • • ▬
E •	N ▬ •	V • • • ▬
F • • ▬ •	O ▬ ▬ ▬	W • ▬ ▬
G ▬ ▬ •	P • ▬ ▬ •	X ▬ • • ▬
H • • • •	Q ▬ ▬ • ▬	Y ▬ • ▬ ▬
I • •		Z ▬ ▬ • •

ALDIS LAMP
This lamp has been partially dismantled to show the reflector housing.

Front lamp

Reflector

Silvering

Screw

Spring washer

Retaining clip

Night sight

Day sight

Fixing screw

Cartridge (case)

Shutter trigger

Pistol grip

On/off lamp trigger

Casing

Power supply cord

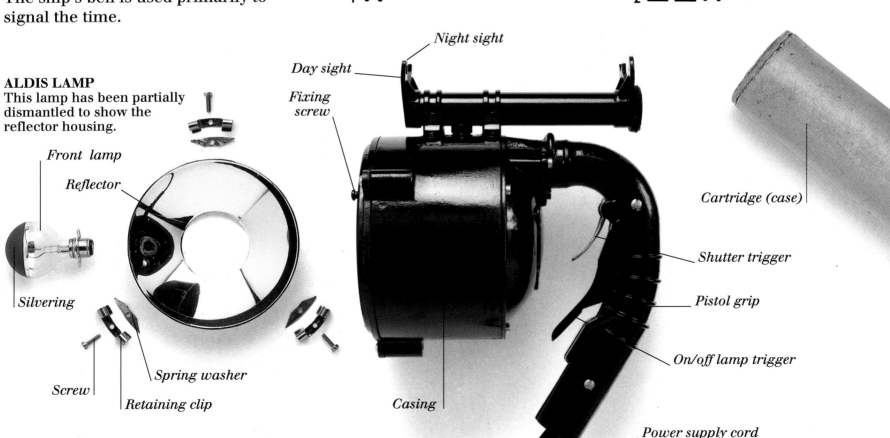

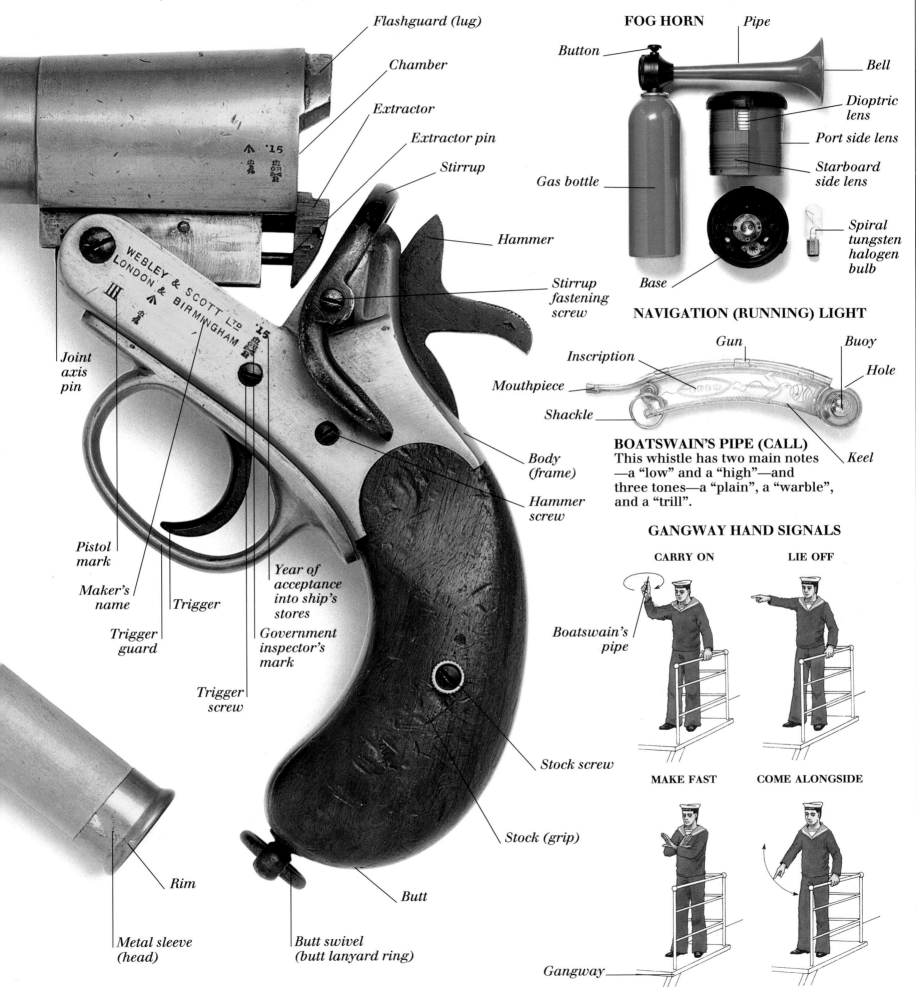

VERY PISTOL (SIGNALING PISTOL)

Flashguard (lug)

Chamber

Extractor

Extractor pin

Stirrup

Hammer

WEBLEY & SCOTT LTD LONDON & BIRMINGHAM '15

Stirrup fastening screw

Joint axis pin

Body (frame)

Hammer screw

Pistol mark

Maker's name

Trigger

Year of acceptance into ship's stores

Government inspector's mark

Trigger guard

Trigger screw

Stock screw

Stock (grip)

Rim

Butt swivel (butt lanyard ring)

Butt

Metal sleeve (head)

FOG HORN

Button

Pipe

Bell

Dioptric lens

Port side lens

Starboard side lens

Gas bottle

Spiral tungsten halogen bulb

Base

NAVIGATION (RUNNING) LIGHT

Gun

Buoy

Hole

Inscription

Mouthpiece

Shackle

Keel

BOATSWAIN'S PIPE (CALL)
This whistle has two main notes —a "low" and a "high"—and three tones—a "plain", a "warble", and a "trill".

GANGWAY HAND SIGNALS

CARRY ON

LIE OFF

Boatswain's pipe

MAKE FAST

COME ALONGSIDE

Gangway

The life raft

IT IS CRUCIAL THAT ALL VESSELS be equipped with the lifesaving gear appropriate to their sailing conditions. The life raft shown here is designed to hold four people in the roughest seas. It inflates quickly, avoids capsizing, and maintains the body heat of those aboard. It should be tied to the ship by a rope called a painter. In an emergency, the crew throws the deflated raft overboard and tugs on the painter, which releases carbon dioxide from a cylinder and inflates the raft. Once aboard, the crew cuts the painter, releases the drogue (sea anchor), opens the emergency pack, and starts looking for land or another ship.

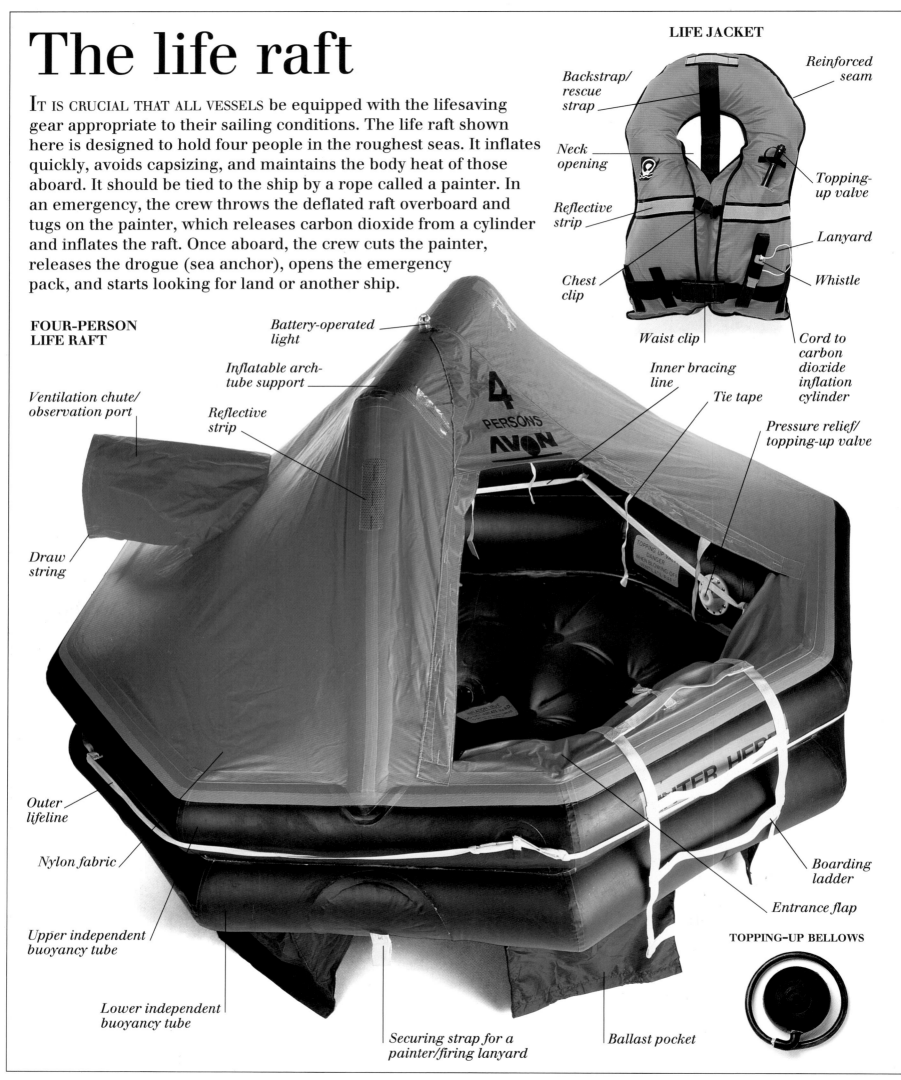

LIFE JACKET

Backstrap/ rescue strap

Reinforced seam

Neck opening

Topping- up valve

Reflective strip

Lanyard

Chest clip

Whistle

Waist clip

Cord to carbon dioxide inflation cylinder

FOUR-PERSON LIFE RAFT

Battery-operated light

Inflatable arch- tube support

Ventilation chute/ observation port

Reflective strip

Inner bracing line

Tie tape

Pressure relief/ topping-up valve

4 PERSONS AVON

Draw string

Outer lifeline

Nylon fabric

Upper independent buoyancy tube

Lower independent buoyancy tube

Securing strap for a painter/firing lanyard

Ballast pocket

Boarding ladder

Entrance flap

TOPPING-UP BELLOWS

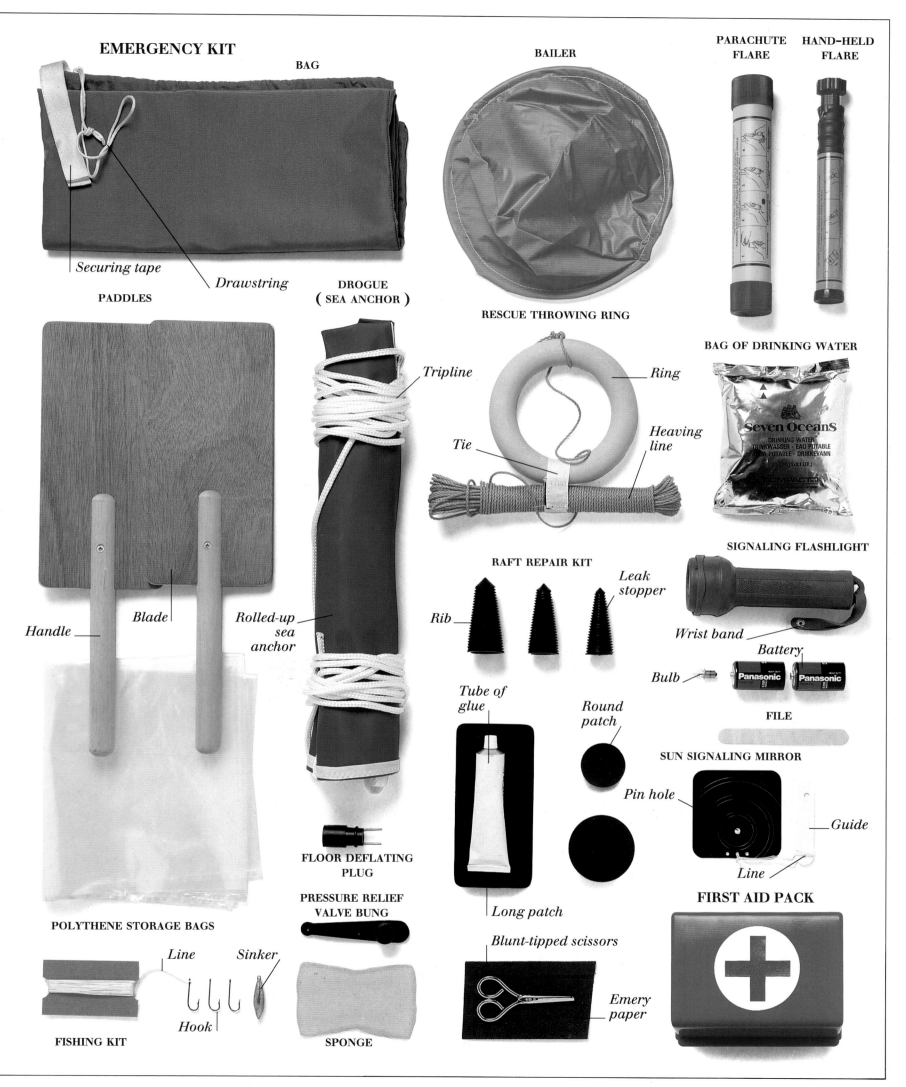

EMERGENCY KIT

BAG

Securing tape

Drawstring

BAILER

PARACHUTE FLARE

HAND-HELD FLARE

PADDLES

DROGUE (SEA ANCHOR)

Tripline

RESCUE THROWING RING

Ring

BAG OF DRINKING WATER

Seven Oceans
DRINKING WATER
TRINKWASSER · EAU POTABLE
AGUA POTABLE · DRIKKEVANN

Tie

Heaving line

Blade

Handle

Rolled-up sea anchor

RAFT REPAIR KIT

Leak stopper

Rib

SIGNALING FLASHLIGHT

Wrist band

Battery

Panasonic   Panasonic

Bulb

FILE

Tube of glue

Round patch

SUN SIGNALING MIRROR

Pin hole

Guide

FLOOR DEFLATING PLUG

Long patch

Line

POLYTHENE STORAGE BAGS

PRESSURE RELIEF VALVE BUNG

FIRST AID PACK

Line

Sinker

Blunt-tipped scissors

Hook

Emery paper

FISHING KIT

SPONGE

Mooring and anchoring

IN MOST HARBORS AND PORTS, a ship can moor (tie up or "make fast") directly to a pier, wharf, or quay (pronounced "key"), using heavy hawsers and docking lines attached to bitts or bollards. Hawsers are tied to each other with knots called bends. In open water, however, ships that are not under way must drop an anchor, which attaches the ship securely to the seabed. The earliest anchors were simply heavy stones. Later, various anchor designs were developed for different uses. Most small vessels today use Danforth or plow anchors, which dig deeply into the sea bottom. A permanent mooring is an anchor set in the bottom to which a ship can tie up without using its own anchor. On old sailing ships, anchors were pulled up, or "weighed," by sailors pushing against bars that turned a capstan, which wound up the anchor cable. Now, most capstans are powered by electricity.

STONE ANCHOR (KILLICK)

Rope hole

TYPES OF ANCHOR

CLOSE-STOWING ANCHOR

CQR ANCHOR (PLOW ANCHOR)

BRITISH ADMIRALTY ANCHOR TYPE ACII

YACHTSMAN'S ANCHOR (KEDGE)

STOCKLESS ANCHOR

MUSHROOM ANCHOR (PERMANENT MOORING ANCHOR)

ANCHOR CHAIN

End link | *Common link* | *Patent link*

SHACKLE, SWIVELS, AND LINK

Crown

Bolt | *Lug* | *Screw thread*

GALVANIZED "D" SHACKLE | **MOORING SWIVEL** | **CHAIN SWIVEL** | **SCREW LINK**

DANFORTH ANCHOR

Shank

Pea (bill)

Fluke (palm)

Throat

Stock

Tripping palm | *Crown*

TWIN BOLLARDS (BITTS), WITH RAKED PILLARS AND A HAWSER (HEAVY ROPE)

Flat

Rim

Base

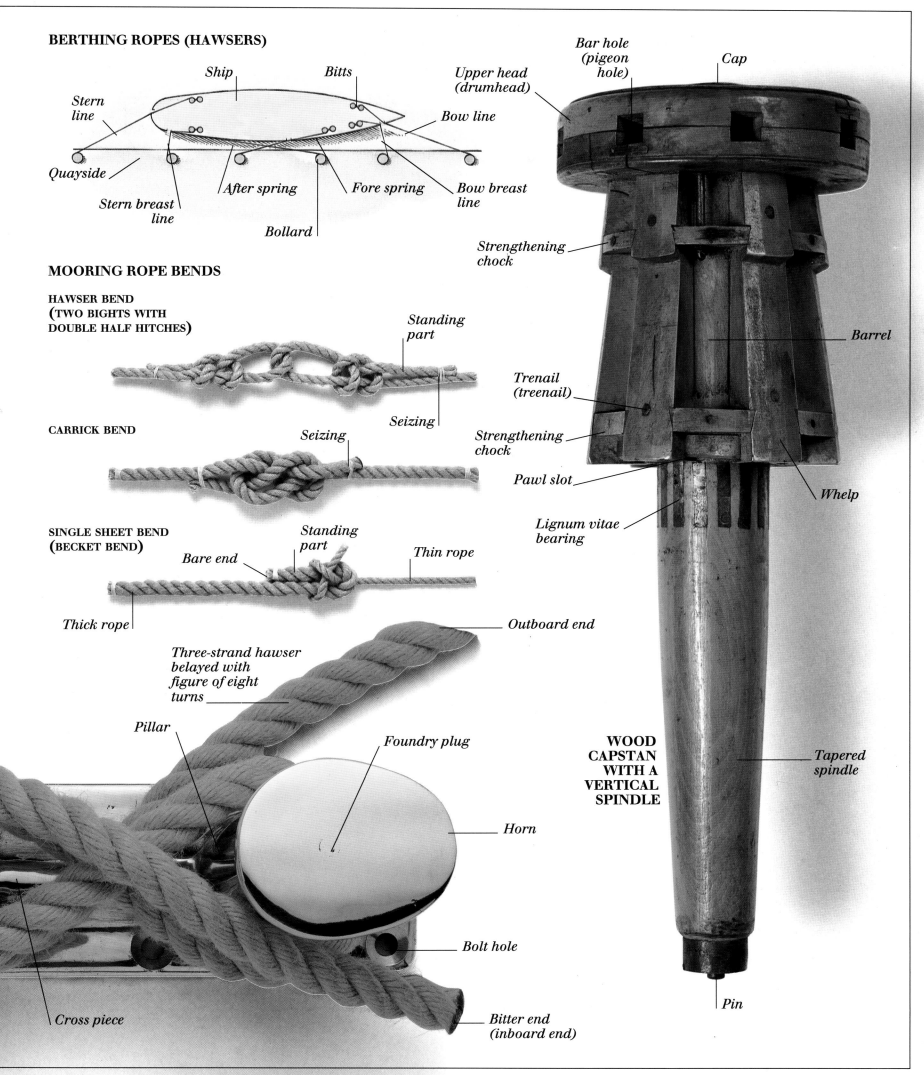

BERTHING ROPES (HAWSERS)

Ship

Bitts

Bar hole (pigeon hole)

Cap

Stern line

Upper head (drumhead)

Bow line

Quayside

Strengthening chock

After spring

Fore spring

Bow breast line

Stern breast line

Bollard

Barrel

MOORING ROPE BENDS

HAWSER BEND (TWO BIGHTS WITH DOUBLE HALF HITCHES)

Standing part

Seizing

Trenail (treenail)

Strengthening chock

CARRICK BEND

Seizing

Pawl slot

Whelp

Lignum vitae bearing

SINGLE SHEET BEND (BECKET BEND)

Standing part

Thin rope

Bare end

Thick rope

Outboard end

Three-strand hawser belayed with figure of eight turns

Pillar

Foundry plug

WOOD CAPSTAN WITH A VERTICAL SPINDLE

Tapered spindle

Horn

Bolt hole

Pin

Cross piece

Bitter end (inboard end)

Ropes and knots

ALL KINDS OF ROPES ARE USED AT SEA, from thin twines and yarn to thick hawsers. Synthetic fibers are much in use today. Nylon ropes stretch, and so are ideal for anchoring; polyester (frequently called by the trade name Dacron) has little stretch and is used for halyards and sheets. Different knots have different uses. Knots that join two ropes are often called bends; hitches join a rope to another object. Ropes, usually called "lines" on board ship, can also be joined by seizing (lashing them together side by side) or splicing (unraveling the ends and weaving them together).

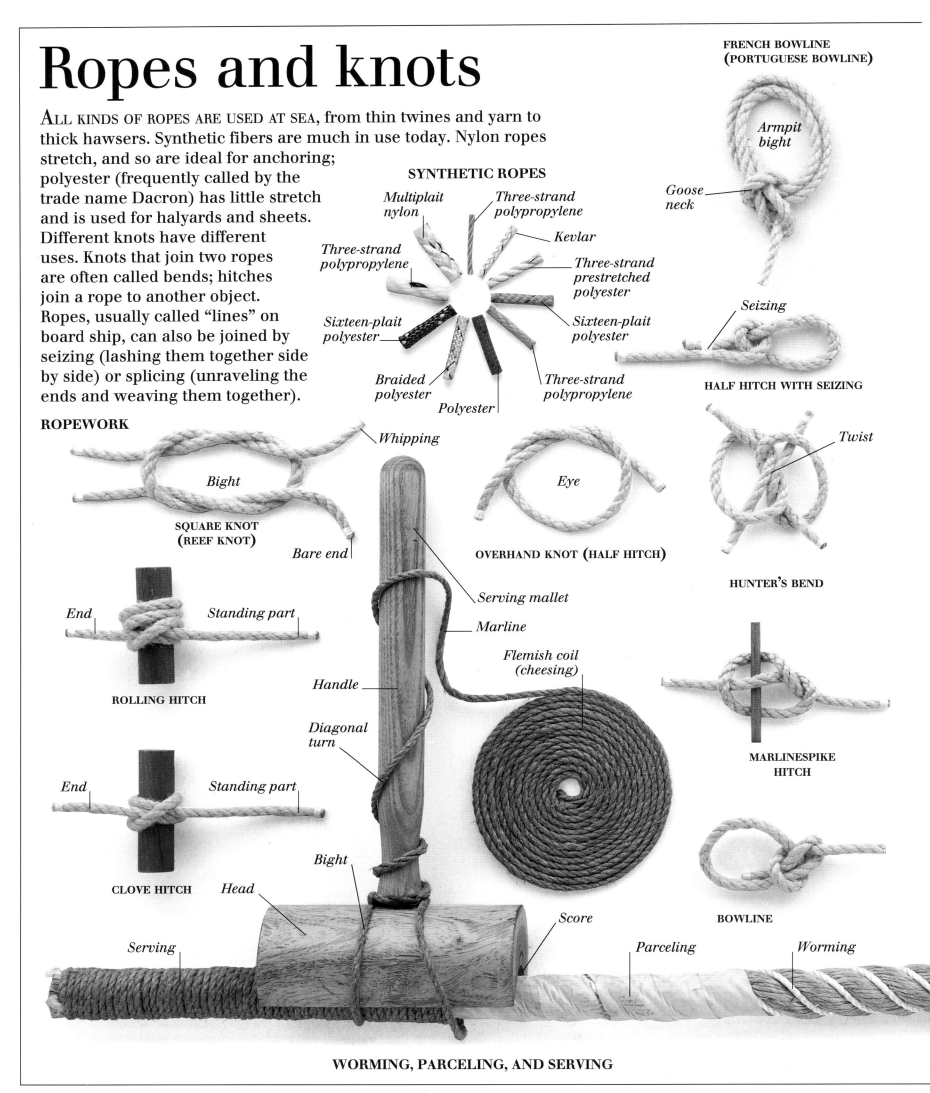

FRENCH BOWLINE (PORTUGUESE BOWLINE)

Armpit bight

Goose neck

SYNTHETIC ROPES

Multiplait nylon

Three-strand polypropylene

Kevlar

Three-strand polypropylene

Three-strand prestretched polyester

Sixteen-plait polyester

Sixteen-plait polyester

Braided polyester

Polyester

Three-strand polypropylene

Seizing

HALF HITCH WITH SEIZING

ROPEWORK

Whipping

Bight

SQUARE KNOT (REEF KNOT)

Bare end

Eye

OVERHAND KNOT (HALF HITCH)

Twist

HUNTER'S BEND

End

Standing part

ROLLING HITCH

Serving mallet

Marline

Flemish coil (cheesing)

MARLINESPIKE HITCH

End

Standing part

CLOVE HITCH

Handle

Diagonal turn

Bight

Head

Score

BOWLINE

Serving

Parceling

Worming

WORMING, PARCELING, AND SERVING

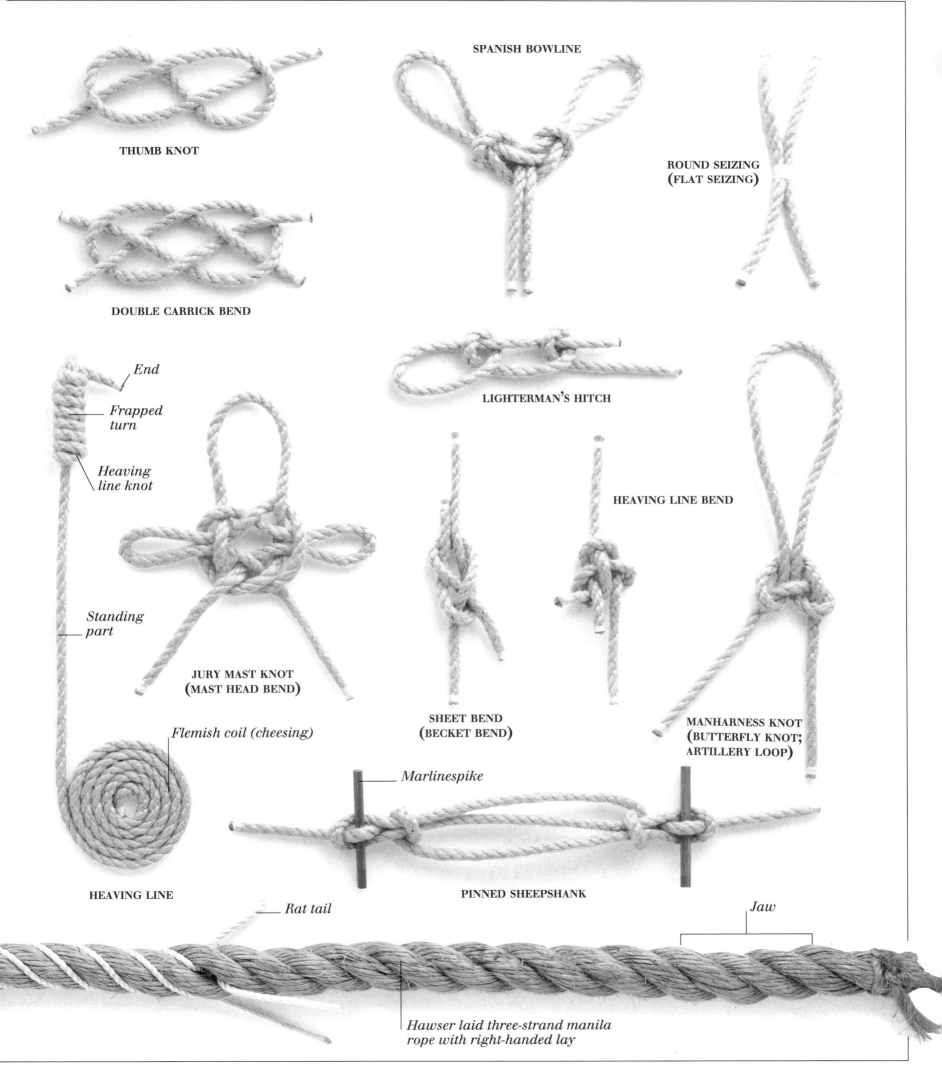

THUMB KNOT

SPANISH BOWLINE

**ROUND SEIZING
(FLAT SEIZING)**

DOUBLE CARRICK BEND

End

Frapped turn

Heaving line knot

Standing part

LIGHTERMAN'S HITCH

HEAVING LINE BEND

**JURY MAST KNOT
(MAST HEAD BEND)**

Flemish coil (cheesing)

**SHEET BEND
(BECKET BEND)**

**MANHARNESS KNOT
(BUTTERFLY KNOT;
ARTILLERY LOOP)**

Marlinespike

Jaw

HEAVING LINE

PINNED SHEEPSHANK

Rat tail

*Hawser laid three-strand manila
rope with right-handed lay*

Sailing clothing

THE PRINCIPAL FUNCTIONS OF SAILING CLOTHING are to maintain body temperature, be waterproof, and allow freedom of movement. The clothing shown is intended for long distance and foul-weather sailing. Water and wind both contribute to loss of body heat, and modern sailing clothing protects the body efficiently by allowing the formation of a layer of warm air around the body. The materials used must be lightweight and quick-drying. This jacket has numerous safety features, including life jacket, safety harness, whistle, and a pocket for emergency flares.

GLOVE

Water-resistant leather palm

Removable lining

Anti-seasickness wrist band

Adjustable storm cuff

High-intensity strobe light

OCEAN-SAILING TROUSERS

Suspenders

Webbing

Carabiner (double-action safety hook)

Life jacket pull tag

Chest-high handwarmer pocket

ACCESSORIES

Nylon safety line

Heavy-duty zipper

HAND WARMER

KNIFE AND SHEATH

Handle

Metal casing

SHACKLE PIN OPENER

Thigh pocket

Charcoal

Eye

Nylon reinforcement

Zinc cream

Marlinespike

Applicator

Sheath

Blade

DECK BOOT

SUN PROTECTION

DECK SHOES

Oiled leather upper

Watertight adjustable collar

Rot-proof synthetic thread

Nonslip sole

Adjustable ankle fastener

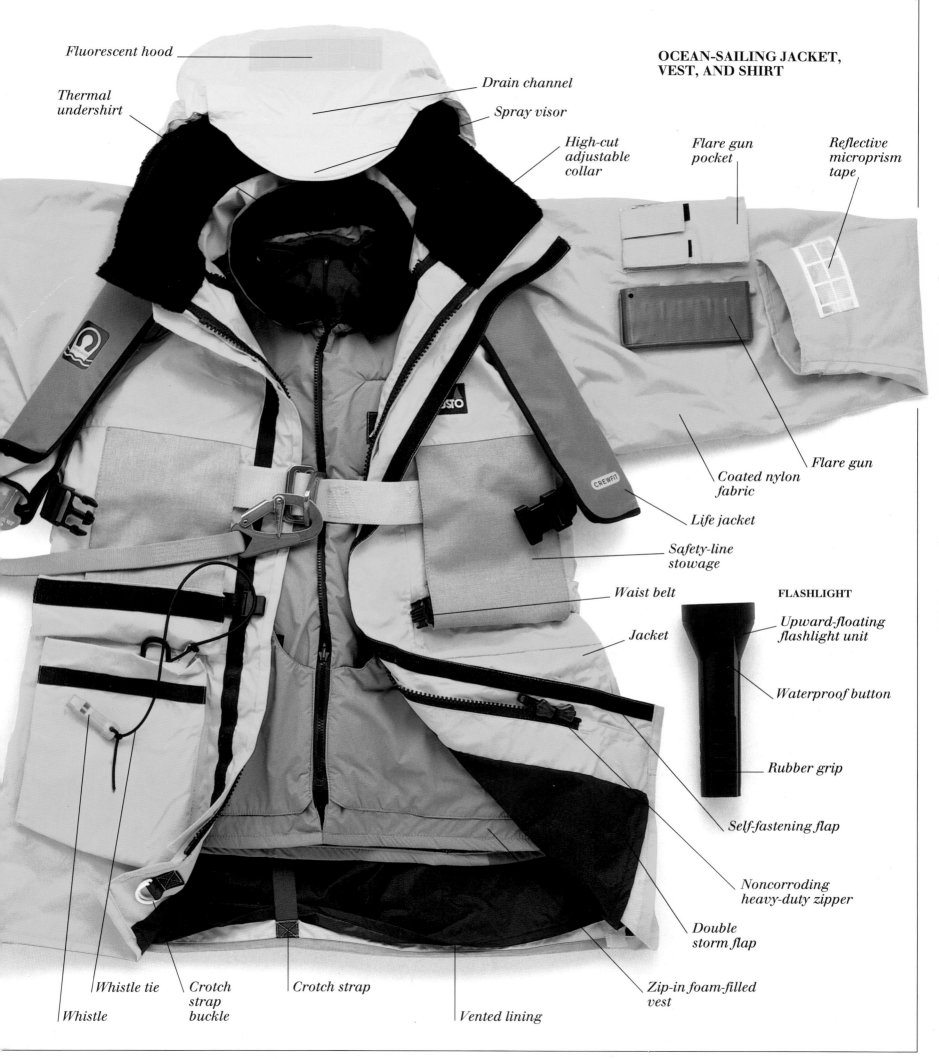

Fluorescent hood

Thermal
undershirt

Drain channel

Spray visor

High-cut
adjustable
collar

**OCEAN-SAILING JACKET,
VEST, AND SHIRT**

Flare gun
pocket

Reflective
microprism
tape

Flare gun

Coated nylon
fabric

Life jacket

Safety-line
stowage

Waist belt

Jacket

FLASHLIGHT

Upward-floating
flashlight unit

Waterproof button

Rubber grip

Self-fastening flap

Noncorroding
heavy-duty zipper

Double
storm flap

Zip-in foam-filled
vest

Whistle tie

Whistle

Crotch
strap
buckle

Crotch strap

Vented lining

The battleship

In the early years of the 20th century, sea warfare—attacking enemy vessels or defending a ship—was revolutionized by the introduction of Dreadnought-type battleships like the Brazilian vessel below. These new ships combined the latest advances in steam propulsion, gunnery, and armor plating. Their gun turrets, protected by armor up to 12 in (30 cm) thick, were designed to fire shells over great distances. The ship shown here, the Minas Geraes, was 500 ft (152 m) long. It was built at Elswick, England, and launched in 1908. Its chief armament was of 12 in (30 cm) guns (firing shells with a 12 in diameter). Other naval weapons developed in the 20th century include the torpedo—as portrayed on the upper cigarette card (right). This was a self-propelled underwater missile, often steered by gyro-control. Depth charges were designed in the First World War for use against submerged U-boats. They are canisters filled with explosives that are detonated by depth-sensitive pistols. The lower cigarette card shows depth charges being fired by a "thrower", fired from a torpedo tube, and rolled from the stern. Ship's shields were fitted to warships from the late 19th century onwards. The shield shown opposite depicts a traditional ship's cannon.

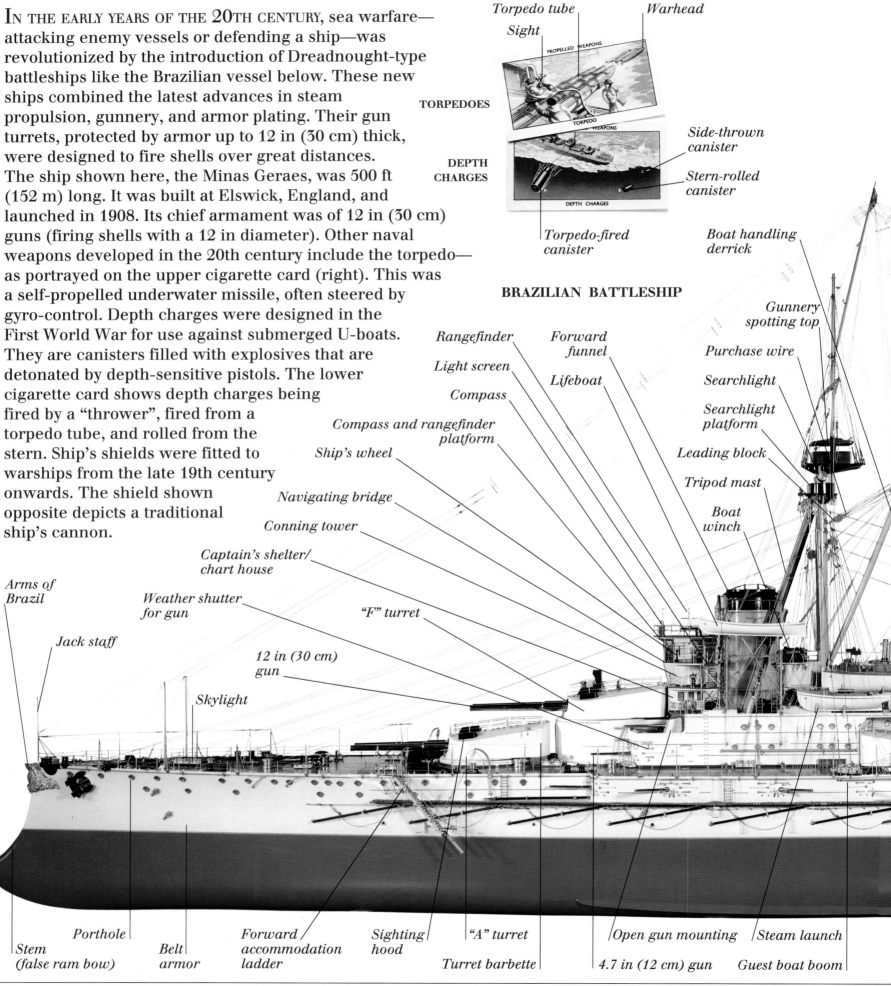

Torpedo tube   Warhead
Sight

TORPEDOES

DEPTH CHARGES

Side-thrown canister

Stern-rolled canister

Torpedo-fired canister

Boat handling derrick

BRAZILIAN BATTLESHIP

Rangefinder   Forward funnel

Light screen

Lifeboat

Compass

Compass and rangefinder platform

Ship's wheel

Navigating bridge

Conning tower

Captain's shelter/ chart house

Weather shutter for gun

"F" turret

12 in (30 cm) gun

Arms of Brazil

Jack staff

Skylight

Gunnery spotting top

Purchase wire

Searchlight

Searchlight platform

Leading block

Tripod mast

Boat winch

Stem (false ram bow)

Porthole

Belt armor

Forward accommodation ladder

Sighting hood

"A" turret

Turret barbette

Open gun mounting

4.7 in (12 cm) gun

Steam launch

Guest boat boom

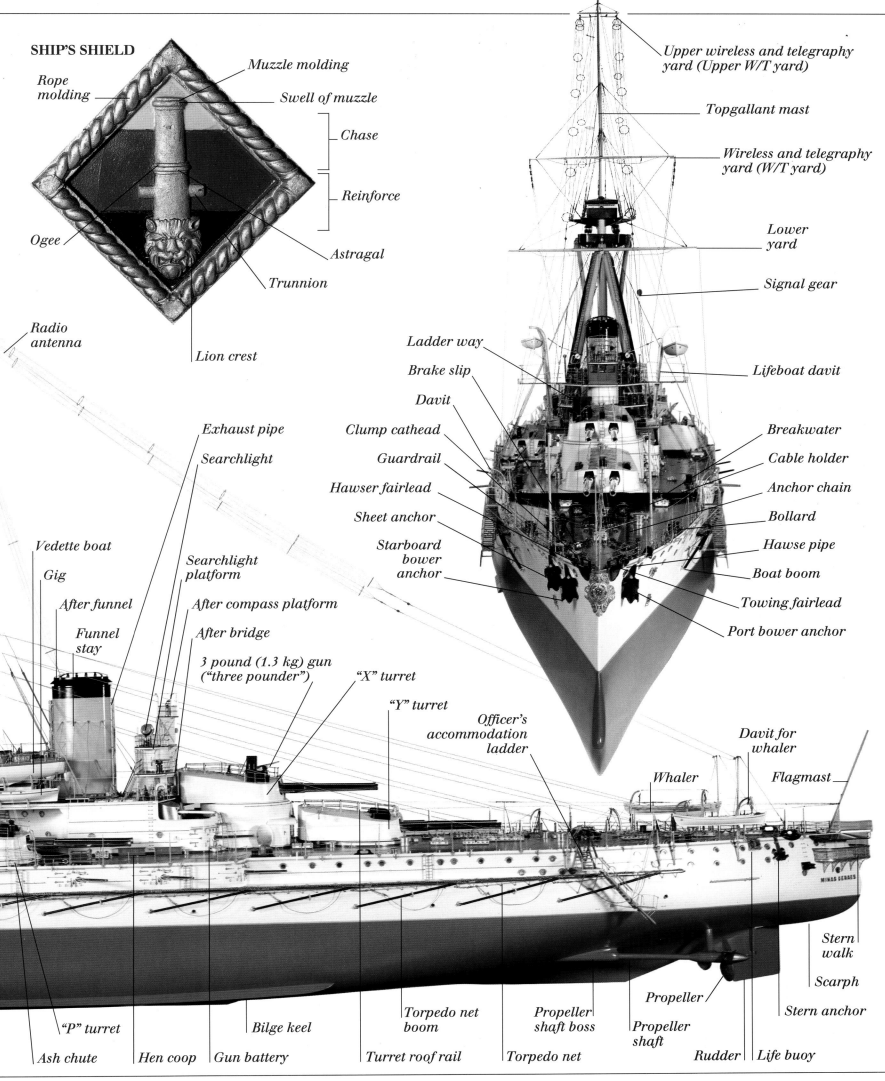

SHIP'S SHIELD

Rope molding

Muzzle molding

Swell of muzzle

Chase

Reinforce

Ogee

Astragal

Trunnion

Lion crest

Radio antenna

Upper wireless and telegraphy yard (Upper W/T yard)

Topgallant mast

Wireless and telegraphy yard (W/T yard)

Lower yard

Signal gear

Ladder way

Brake slip

Davit

Clump cathead

Guardrail

Hawser fairlead

Sheet anchor

Starboard bower anchor

Lifeboat davit

Breakwater

Cable holder

Anchor chain

Bollard

Hawse pipe

Boat boom

Towing fairlead

Port bower anchor

Exhaust pipe

Searchlight

Vedette boat

Gig

After funnel

Funnel stay

Searchlight platform

After compass platform

After bridge

3 pound (1.3 kg) gun ("three pounder")

"X" turret

"Y" turret

Officer's accommodation ladder

Davit for whaler

Whaler

Flagmast

Stern walk

Scarph

Stern anchor

"P" turret

Ash chute

Hen coop

Bilge keel

Gun battery

Torpedo net boom

Turret roof rail

Propeller shaft boss

Torpedo net

Propeller shaft

Propeller

Rudder

Life buoy

53

Fighting at sea

From the mid-19th century, armored ships provided a new challenge to enemy craft. In response, huge revolving gun turrets were developed. These could shoot in any direction, were loaded quickly from the breech, and fired exploding shells. Today's fighting ships, like the Royal Navy frigate opposite, also carry missile launchers and helicopters. Submarines operate underwater, have great speed, and some can fire missiles while submerged. A nuclear sub can operate for several years without refueling.

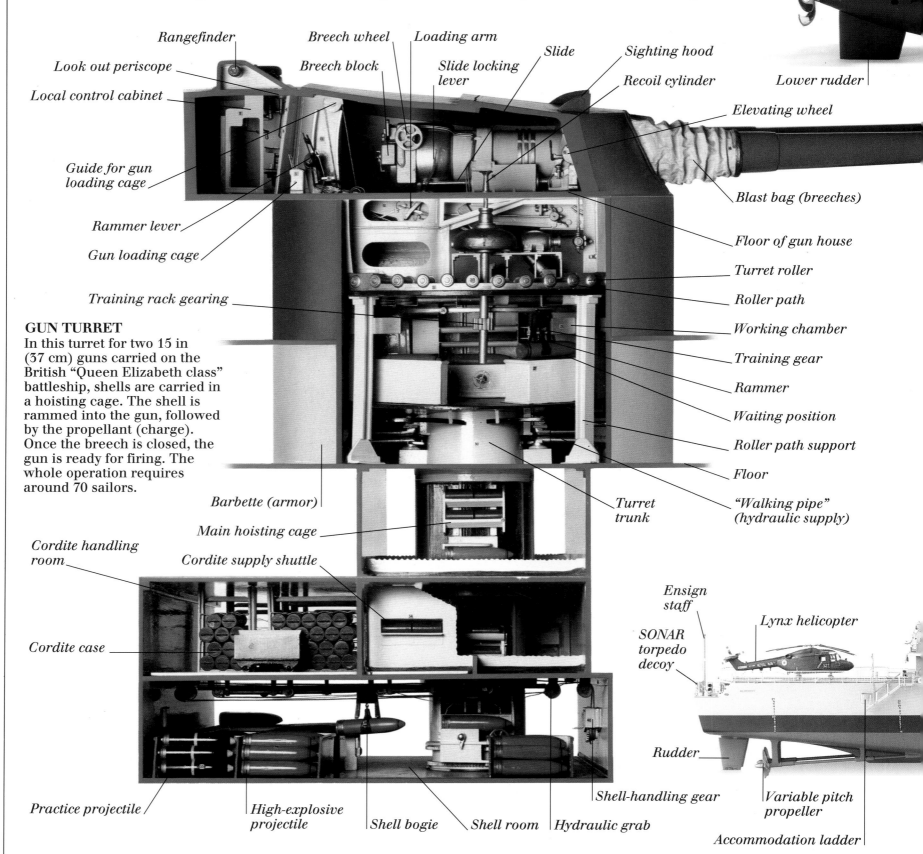

Rangefinder

Look out periscope

Local control cabinet

Breech wheel

Breech block

Loading arm

Slide locking lever

Slide

Sighting hood

Recoil cylinder

Stabilized fin

Aft hydroplane

Propeller

Lower rudder

Elevating wheel

Guide for gun loading cage

Rammer lever

Gun loading cage

Training rack gearing

Blast bag (breeches)

Floor of gun house

Turret roller

Roller path

Working chamber

Training gear

Rammer

Waiting position

Roller path support

Floor

"Walking pipe" (hydraulic supply)

GUN TURRET
In this turret for two 15 in (37 cm) guns carried on the British "Queen Elizabeth class" battleship, shells are carried in a hoisting cage. The shell is rammed into the gun, followed by the propellant (charge). Once the breech is closed, the gun is ready for firing. The whole operation requires around 70 sailors.

Barbette (armor)

Main hoisting cage

Cordite handling room

Cordite supply shuttle

Cordite case

Turret trunk

Ensign staff

SONAR torpedo decoy

Lynx helicopter

Rudder

Practice projectile

High-explosive projectile

Shell bogie

Shell room

Hydraulic grab

Shell-handling gear

Variable pitch propeller

Accommodation ladder

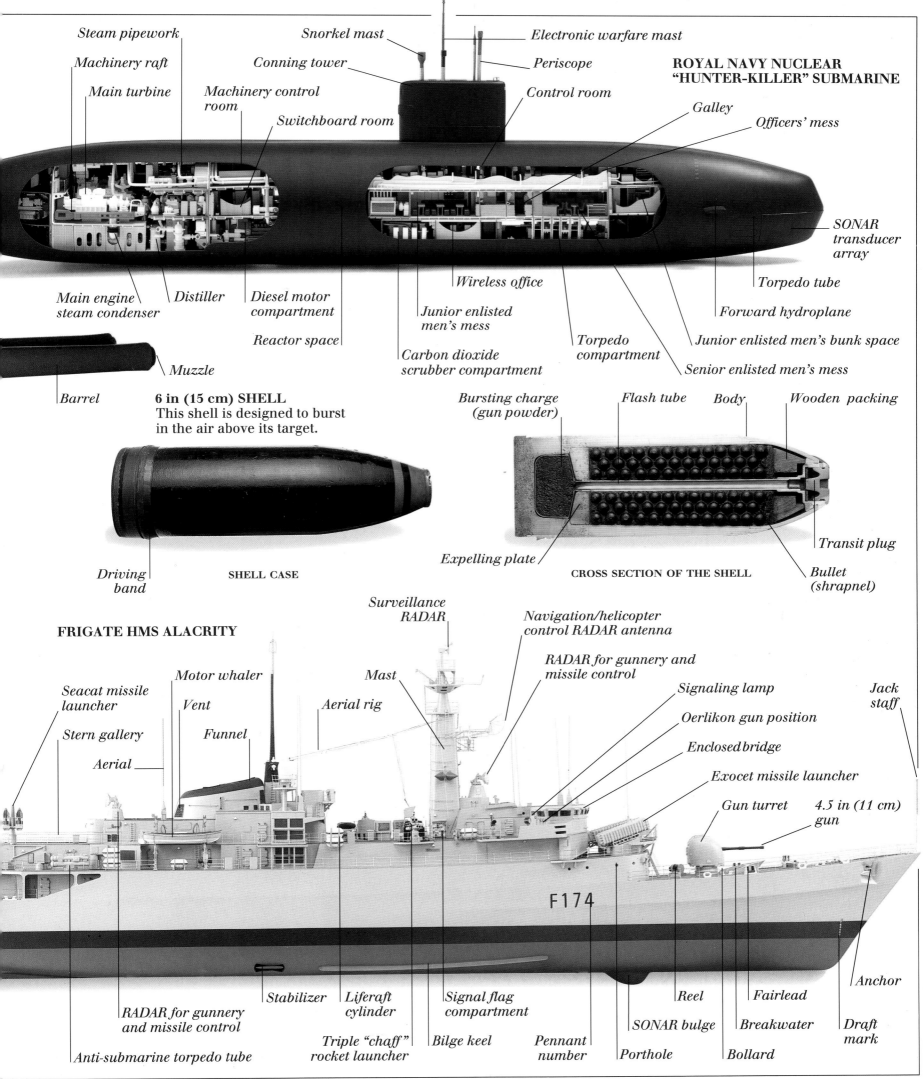

Steam pipework

Machinery raft

Main turbine

Snorkel mast

Conning tower

Machinery control room

Switchboard room

Electronic warfare mast

Periscope

Control room

ROYAL NAVY NUCLEAR "HUNTER-KILLER" SUBMARINE

Galley

Officers' mess

SONAR transducer array

Main engine steam condenser

Distiller

Diesel motor compartment

Reactor space

Muzzle

Barrel

Wireless office

Junior enlisted men's mess

Carbon dioxide scrubber compartment

Torpedo compartment

Torpedo tube

Forward hydroplane

Junior enlisted men's bunk space

Senior enlisted men's mess

6 in (15 cm) SHELL
This shell is designed to burst in the air above its target.

Bursting charge (gun powder)

Flash tube

Body

Wooden packing

Transit plug

Expelling plate

CROSS SECTION OF THE SHELL

Bullet (shrapnel)

Driving band

SHELL CASE

FRIGATE HMS ALACRITY

Surveillance RADAR

Navigation/helicopter control RADAR antenna

RADAR for gunnery and missile control

Signaling lamp

Oerlikon gun position

Enclosed bridge

Exocet missile launcher

Gun turret

4.5 in (11 cm) gun

Jack staff

Seacat missile launcher

Stern gallery

Aerial

Motor whaler

Vent

Funnel

Mast

Aerial rig

F174

Anchor

RADAR for gunnery and missile control

Anti-submarine torpedo tube

Stabilizer

Liferaft cylinder

Triple "chaff" rocket launcher

Signal flag compartment

Bilge keel

Pennant number

Porthole

Reel

SONAR bulge

Fairlead

Bollard

Breakwater

Draft mark

Fishing boats

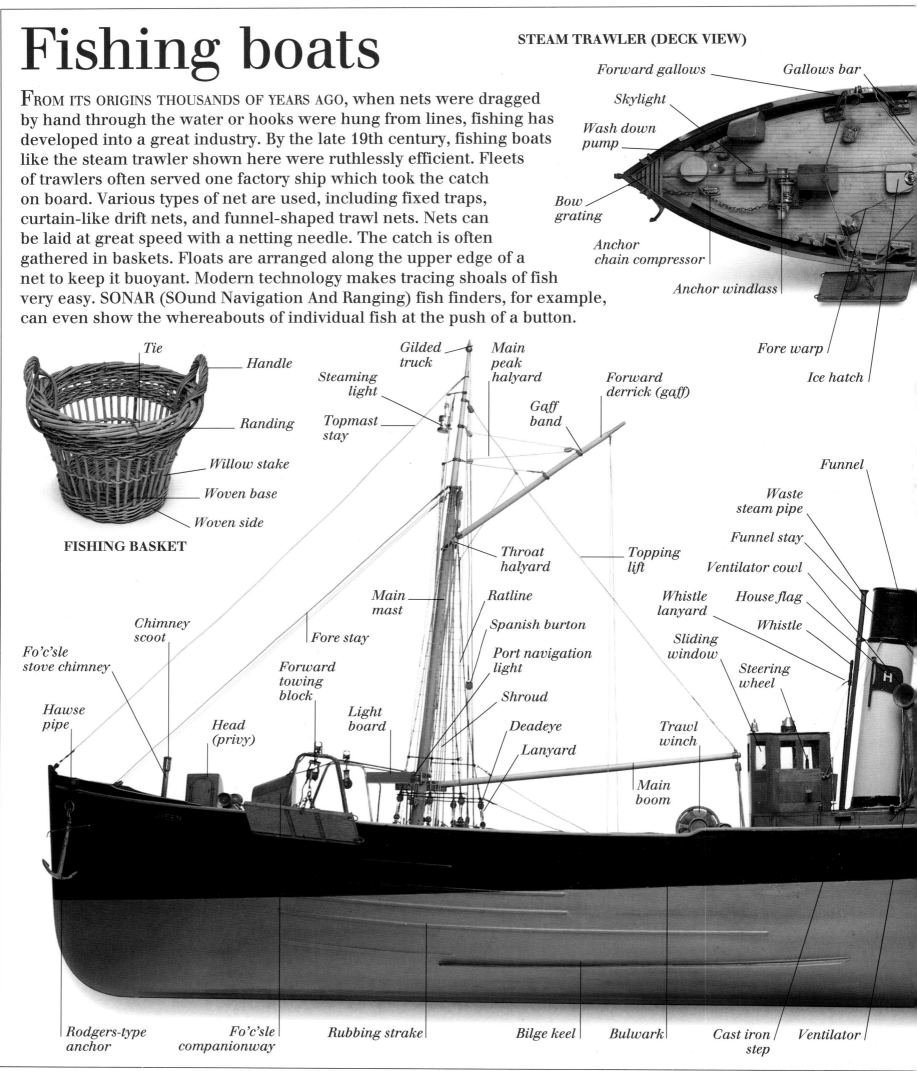

FROM ITS ORIGINS THOUSANDS OF YEARS AGO, when nets were dragged by hand through the water or hooks were hung from lines, fishing has developed into a great industry. By the late 19th century, fishing boats like the steam trawler shown here were ruthlessly efficient. Fleets of trawlers often served one factory ship which took the catch on board. Various types of net are used, including fixed traps, curtain-like drift nets, and funnel-shaped trawl nets. Nets can be laid at great speed with a netting needle. The catch is often gathered in baskets. Floats are arranged along the upper edge of a net to keep it buoyant. Modern technology makes tracing shoals of fish very easy. SONAR (SOund Navigation And Ranging) fish finders, for example, can even show the whereabouts of individual fish at the push of a button.

STEAM TRAWLER (DECK VIEW)

Forward gallows

Gallows bar

Skylight

Wash down pump

Bow grating

Anchor chain compressor

Anchor windlass

Fore warp

Ice hatch

Tie

Handle

Randing

Willow stake

Woven base

Woven side

FISHING BASKET

Gilded truck

Main peak halyard

Steaming light

Topmast stay

Forward derrick (gaff)

Gaff band

Throat halyard

Topping lift

Main mast

Ratline

Spanish burton

Funnel

Waste steam pipe

Funnel stay

Ventilator cowl

House flag

Whistle lanyard

Whistle

Sliding window

Steering wheel

Chimney scoot

Fore stay

Port navigation light

Fo'c'sle stove chimney

Forward towing block

Shroud

Light board

Deadeye

Trawl winch

Hawse pipe

Head (privy)

Lanyard

Main boom

Rodgers-type anchor

Fo'c'sle companionway

Rubbing strake

Bilge keel

Bulwark

Cast iron step

Ventilator

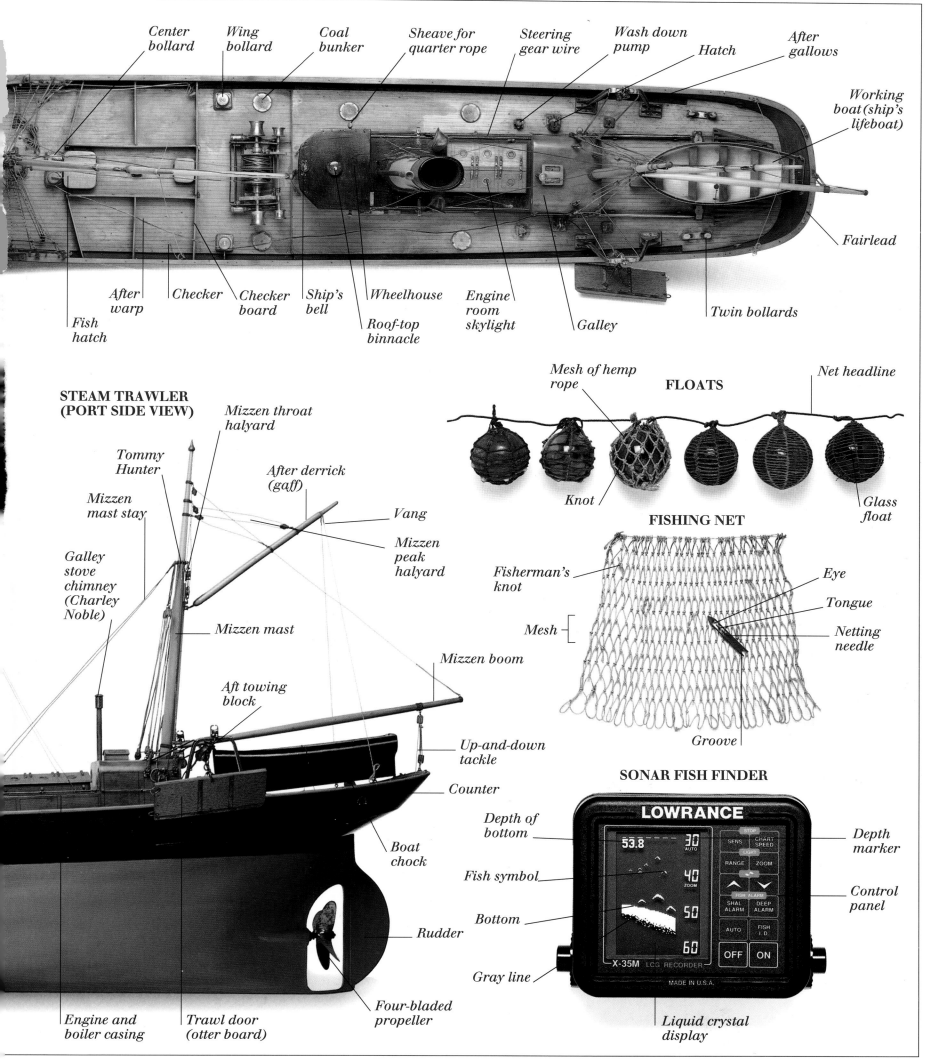

Center bollard

Wing bollard

Coal bunker

Sheave for quarter rope

Steering gear wire

Wash down pump

Hatch

After gallows

Working boat (ship's lifeboat)

Fairlead

After warp

Checker

Checker board

Ship's bell

Wheelhouse

Engine room skylight

Galley

Twin bollards

Fish hatch

Roof-top binnacle

STEAM TRAWLER (PORT SIDE VIEW)

Mizzen throat halyard

Tommy Hunter

After derrick (gaff)

Vang

Mizzen mast stay

Mizzen peak halyard

Mizzen

Galley stove chimney (Charley Noble)

Mizzen mast

Mizzen boom

Aft towing block

Up-and-down tackle

Counter

Boat chock

Rudder

Engine and boiler casing

Trawl door (otter board)

Four-bladed propeller

Mesh of hemp rope

FLOATS

Net headline

Knot

Glass float

FISHING NET

Fisherman's knot

Eye

Tongue

Mesh

Netting needle

Groove

SONAR FISH FINDER

Depth of bottom

Depth marker

LOWRANCE

53.8

30 AUTO

STOP

SENS

CHART SPEED

LIGHT

RANGE

ZOOM

40 ZOOM

FISH ALARM

SHAL ALARM

DEEP ALARM

50

AUTO

FISH I.D.

60

OFF

ON

X-35M LCG RECORDER

MADE IN U.S.A.

Control panel

Fish symbol

Bottom

Gray line

Liquid crystal display

Under the sea

THE EARTH'S LAST FRONTIER IS UNDER THE SEA, and it is also one of the world's most hostile environments for humans. Specialized craft and clothing are needed to protect divers who explore deep under water. Submersibles that can operate at great depths are either manned or remotely controlled. The one shown here carries one pilot, whose lifeline is the umbilical cable that carries power, signals, and video messages back and forth. For divers working outside the relative safety of a submersible, new kinds of equipment—like the heated suit and closed helmet shown here—are continually being developed.

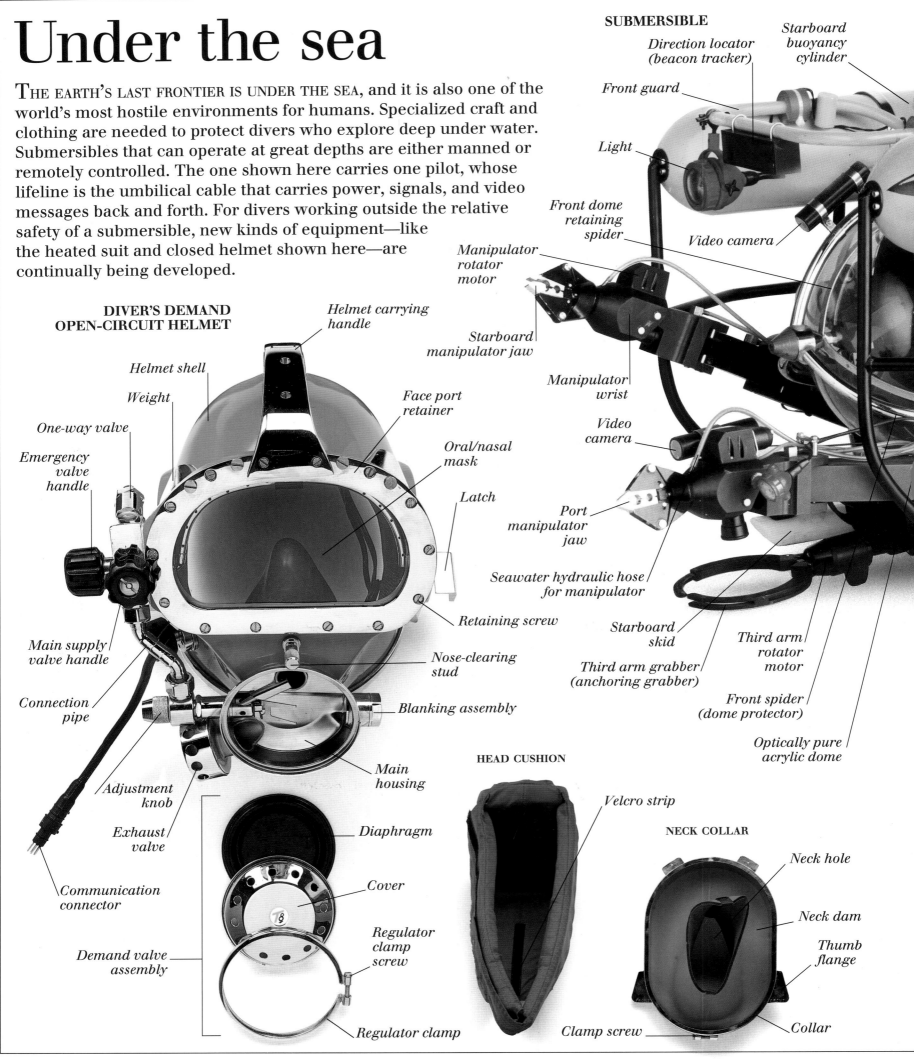

SUBMERSIBLE

Direction locator (beacon tracker)

Starboard buoyancy cylinder

Front guard

Light

Front dome retaining spider

Video camera

Manipulator rotator motor

Starboard manipulator jaw

Manipulator wrist

Video camera

Port manipulator jaw

Seawater hydraulic hose for manipulator

Starboard skid

Third arm grabber (anchoring grabber)

Third arm rotator motor

Front spider (dome protector)

Optically pure acrylic dome

DIVER'S DEMAND OPEN-CIRCUIT HELMET

Helmet carrying handle

Helmet shell

Weight

Face port retainer

One-way valve

Oral/nasal mask

Emergency valve handle

Latch

Main supply valve handle

Retaining screw

Connection pipe

Nose-clearing stud

Adjustment knob

Blanking assembly

Exhaust valve

Main housing

Communication connector

Diaphragm

Cover

Demand valve assembly

Regulator clamp screw

Regulator clamp

HEAD CUSHION

Velcro strip

NECK COLLAR

Neck hole

Neck dam

Thumb flange

Clamp screw

Collar

58

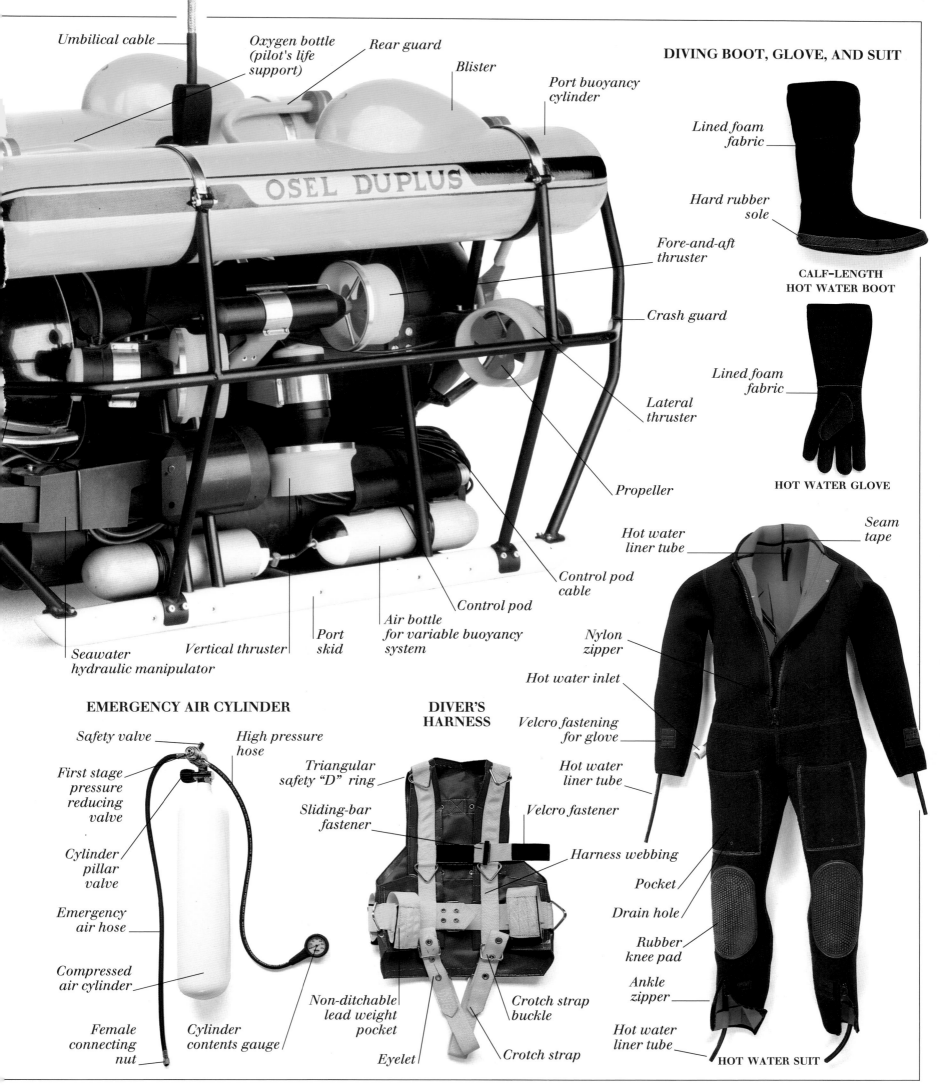

Umbilical cable

Oxygen bottle
(pilot's life
support)

Rear guard

Blister

Port buoyancy
cylinder

OSEL DUPLUS

Fore-and-aft
thruster

Crash guard

Lateral
thruster

Propeller

Control pod
cable

Control pod

Air bottle
for variable buoyancy
system

Port
skid

Vertical thruster

Seawater
hydraulic manipulator

DIVING BOOT, GLOVE, AND SUIT

Lined foam
fabric

Hard rubber
sole

**CALF-LENGTH
HOT WATER BOOT**

Lined foam
fabric

HOT WATER GLOVE

Seam
tape

Hot water
liner tube

Nylon
zipper

Hot water inlet

Velcro fastening
for glove

Hot water
liner tube

Velcro fastener

Harness webbing

Pocket

Drain hole

Rubber
knee pad

Ankle
zipper

Hot water
liner tube

HOT WATER SUIT

EMERGENCY AIR CYLINDER

Safety valve

High pressure
hose

First stage
pressure
reducing
valve

Cylinder
pillar
valve

Emergency
air hose

Compressed
air cylinder

Female
connecting
nut

Cylinder
contents gauge

DIVER'S
HARNESS

Triangular
safety "D" ring

Sliding-bar
fastener

Non-ditchable
lead weight
pocket

Eyelet

Crotch strap
buckle

Crotch strap

Index